ANCIENT HISTORY ATLAS

DISCARD
RETIRÉ

P9-CBH-840

OTHER ATLASES IN THIS SERIES, BY MARTIN GILBERT

American History Atlas
Jewish History Atlas
First World War Atlas
The Arab-Israeli Conflict: Its History in Maps

ANCIENT HISTORY ATLAS

Michael Grant

Cartography by ARTHUR BANKS

Fourth Edition

Weidenfeld and Nicolson
London

© 1971 Michael Grant Publications Ltd
Second edition 1974
Reprinted 1976
Reprinted 1978
Reprinted 1981
Third edition 1986
Fourth edition 1989

All rights reserved. No part of this publication may
be reproduced, stored in a retrieval system, or
transmitted, in any form or by any means, electronic,
mechanical, photocopying, recording or otherwise,
without the prior permission of the publishers.

Weidenfeld and Nicolson Ltd
91 Clapham High Street, London SW4 7TA

ISBN 0 297 79549 X Paperback
Printed in Great Britain by
Redwood Burn Ltd, Trowbridge, Wiltshire

Preface

This is, in the first place, an atlas of the classical world – the ancient Greek and Roman world, which needs to be understood if we are to understand the world of today. To say that such an atlas could ever be a substitute for a historical survey would be an exaggeration. Nevertheless, geography is such a vital, indeed predominant, factor in ancient history – and such a difficult factor because of all the changes of names[1] – that the whole course of events often seems to mean practically nothing without maps, and without a lot of them, carefully devised.

Older classical atlases, apart from a varying degree of emphasis on physical aspects, tended to concentrate on political themes, and it is true enough that these stand in great need of maps. But the present volume attempts to cast the net wider, and to introduce economic, cultural, religious and other topics as well. There are also a number of town plans.

Modern research in archaeology and other fields has shown that the classical world cannot be grasped without some appreciation of what went before it. I have consequently started this book with a number of maps illustrating the Mediterranean world during the second millennium BC, and particularly during the period from 1700 BC onwards, when the international scene had already assumed a well-defined and complex appearance; and the story is carried onwards to offer brief illustrations of the Old Testament. At the other end of the story, the traditional terminal date of the ancient world, the year AD 476 when the last western emperor ceased to reign, is again not a very meaningful landmark, so I have carried on the tale until the reign of Justinian in the following century.

It will be clear enough what a very great deal is owed to the talent of Mr Arthur Banks for transcribing the written and spoken word into cartographic form. I am also most grateful to Mr Julian Shuckburgh for all the assistance he has rendered on behalf of the publishers, and I want to thank Miss Jane Dorner for assistance with the index and Mr C. R. B. Elliott for help with an earlier revised edition. Finally, I have to acknowledge a substantial debt to existing classical atlases, German and English. And I must single out, for a special word of gratitude, the *Atlas of the Classical World* edited by A. A. M. van der Heyden and H. H. Scullard for Messrs Nelson, and *Westermanns Grosser Atlas zur Weltgeshchichte* (Westermann, Braunschweig). N. G. L. Hammond's *Atlas of the Greek and Roman World in Antiquity* (Noyes Press, Park Ridge) is now fundamental.

1971, 1974, 1985, 1988   MICHAEL GRANT

[1] Modern names are given after the ancient in the Index.

List of Maps

Scale: 0 — 100 Miles

Kuban

BLACK SEA

Maikop

Burials c. 2300

TROY
Dorak
Sangarios
Halys
HATTUSAS
Alacahüyük
Alisarhüyük
HITTITES
Kanesh
Keban
Malatya

BEYCESULTAN
Maeander
Miletus
Aphrodisias
Can Hasan
ADANA
Karatepe
Edessa
Mersin
Tarsus
CARCHEMISH
Haran
AMIK
Alalakh
Euphrates
ALEPPO

CYPRUS
Ugarit
Orontes
Hamath
Idalium
Kadesh
QATNA
Homs

BYBLOS

Damascus

HAZOR
Dan
S y r i a n
Megiddo
D e s e r t
Gezer
Gaza
Hebron

Nile
HYKSOS
EGYPT
MEMPHIS

1

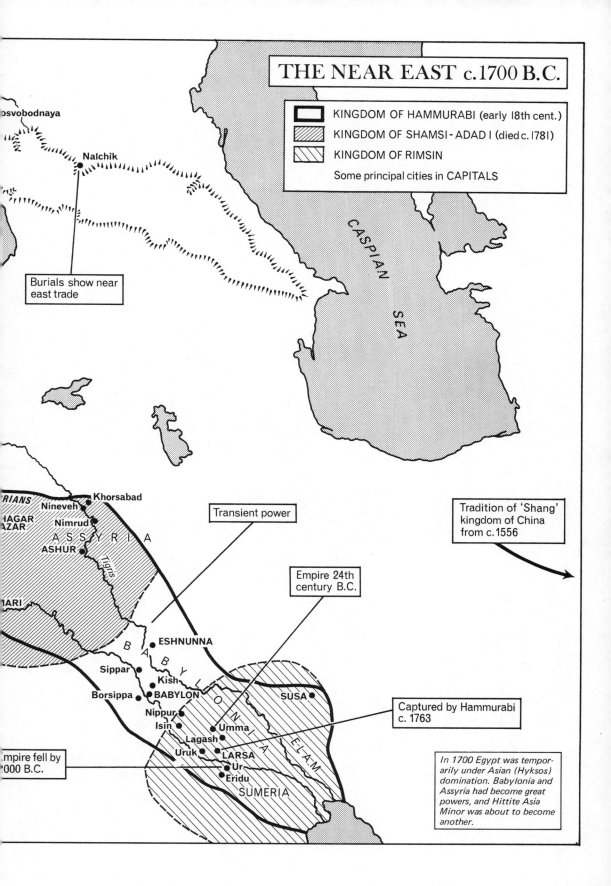

THE NEAR EAST c.1700 B.C.

▭ KINGDOM OF HAMMURABI (early 18th cent.)

▨ KINGDOM OF SHAMSI - ADAD I (died c.1781)

▨ KINGDOM OF RIMSIN

Some principal cities in CAPITALS

Nalchik

svobodnaya

CASPIAN SEA

Burials show near
east trade

Tradition of 'Shang'
kingdom of China
from c.1556

RIANS

Khorsabad

Nineveh

HAGAR
AZAR

Nimrud

A S S Y R I A

ASHUR

Transient power

Empire 24th
century B.C.

MARI

Tigris

B A B Y
L O N
I A

ESHNUNNA

Sippar

Kish

Borsippa   BABYLON

SUSA

Captured by Hammurabi
c. 1763

Nippur

Isin

Umma

E L A M

Lagash

Uruk   LARSA

mpire fell by
000 B.C.

Ur

Eridu

SUMERIA

In 1700 Egypt was tempor-
arily under Asian (Hyksos)
domination. Babylonia and
Assyria had become great
powers, and Hittite Asia
Minor was about to become
another.

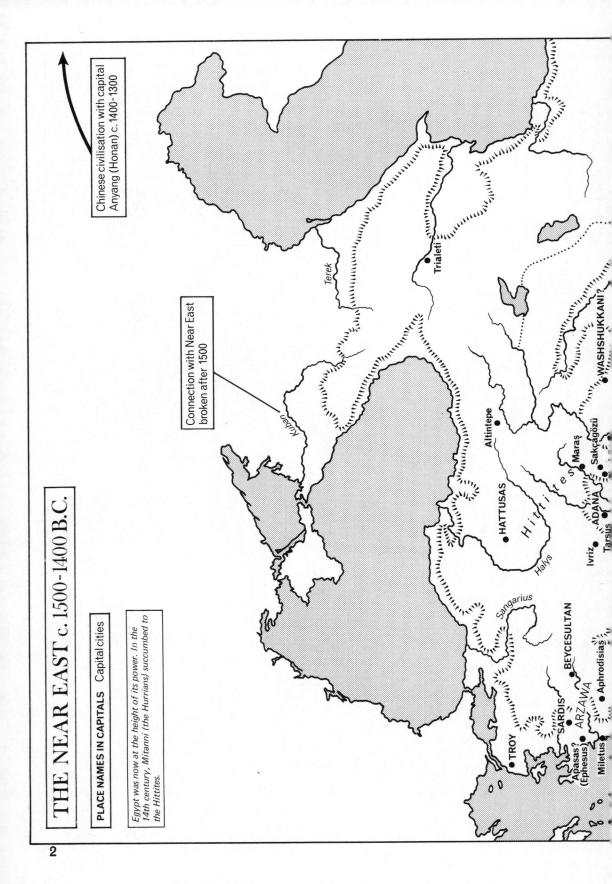

THE NEAR EAST c. 1500-1400 B.C.

PLACE NAMES IN CAPITALS Capital cities

Egypt was now at the height of its power. In the 14th century, Mitanni (the Hurrians) succumbed to the Hittites.

Chinese civilisation with capital Anyang (Honan) c. 1400-1300

Connection with Near East broken after 1500

Terek

Kuban

Trialeti

Altintepe

HATTUSAS

Halys

H i t t i t e s

Maraş

Sakçagözü

ADANA

Tarsus

Ivriz

WASHSHUKKANI?

Sangarius

BEYCESULTAN

SARDIS

ARZAWA

Aphrodisias?

TROY

Apasas?
(Ephesus)

Miletus

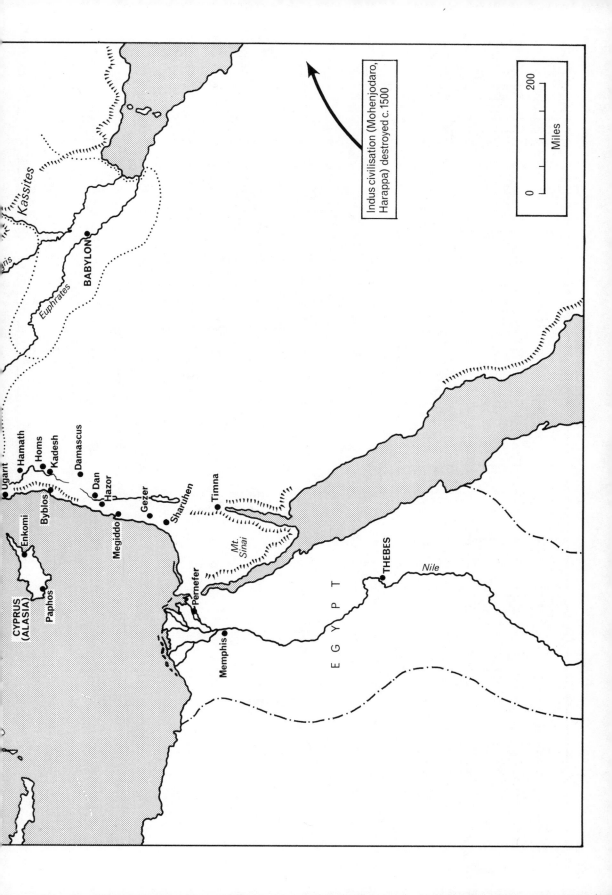

Indus civilisation (Mohenjodaro, Harappa) destroyed c. 1500

200

Miles

0

Kassites

Tigris

Euphrates

BABYLON

Hamath
Homs
Kadesh
Damascus
Ugarit
Byblos
Dan
Hazor
Gezer
Sharuhen
Timna

Enkomi

CYPRUS
(ALASIA)

Paphos

Megiddo

*Mt.
Sinai*

Pernefer

Memphis

E G Y P T

THEBES

Nile

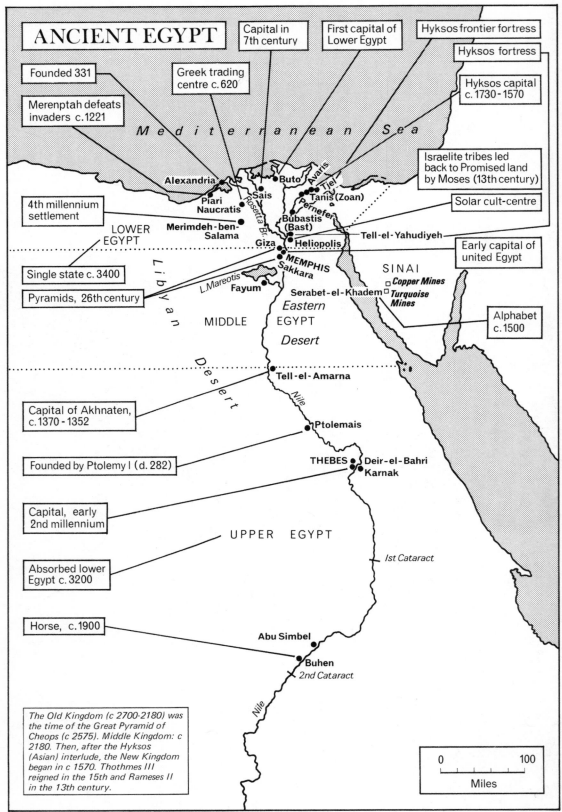

ANCIENT EGYPT

Capital in 7th century

First capital of Lower Egypt

Hyksos frontier fortress

Hyksos fortress

Founded 331

Greek trading centre c. 620

Hyksos capital c. 1730 - 1570

Merenptah defeats invaders c.1221

Mediterranean Sea

Israelite tribes led back to Promised land by Moses (13th century)

4th millennium settlement

Alexandria

Buto

Avaris

Tjel

Piari
Naucratis

Sais

Tanis (Zoan)

Pernefer

Solar cult-centre

LOWER EGYPT

Merimdeh - ben-Salama

Bubastis (Bast)

Tell - el - Yahudiyeh

Single state c. 3400

Rosetta Br.

Giza

Heliopolis

Early capital of united Egypt

Pyramids, 26th century

MEMPHIS
Sakkara

SINAI

L. Mareotis

Fayum

□ *Copper Mines*
□ *Turquoise Mines*

L i b y a n

MIDDLE

Serabet - el - Khadem

Eastern

EGYPT

Alphabet c. 1500

Desert

D e s e r t

Tell - el - Amarna

Capital of Akhnaten, c. 1370 - 1352

Nile

Ptolemais

Founded by Ptolemy I (d. 282)

THEBES **Deir - el - Bahri**

Karnak

Capital, early 2nd millennium

UPPER EGYPT

Absorbed lower Egypt c. 3200

1st Cataract

Horse, c. 1900

Abu Simbel

Buhen

2nd Cataract

Nile

The Old Kingdom (c 2700-2180) was the time of the Great Pyramid of Cheops (c 2575). Middle Kingdom: c 2180. Then, after the Hyksos (Asian) interlude, the New Kingdom began in c 1570. Thothmes III reigned in the 15th and Rameses II in the 13th century.

0   100

Miles

3

MINOAN CRETE AND THE AEGEAN

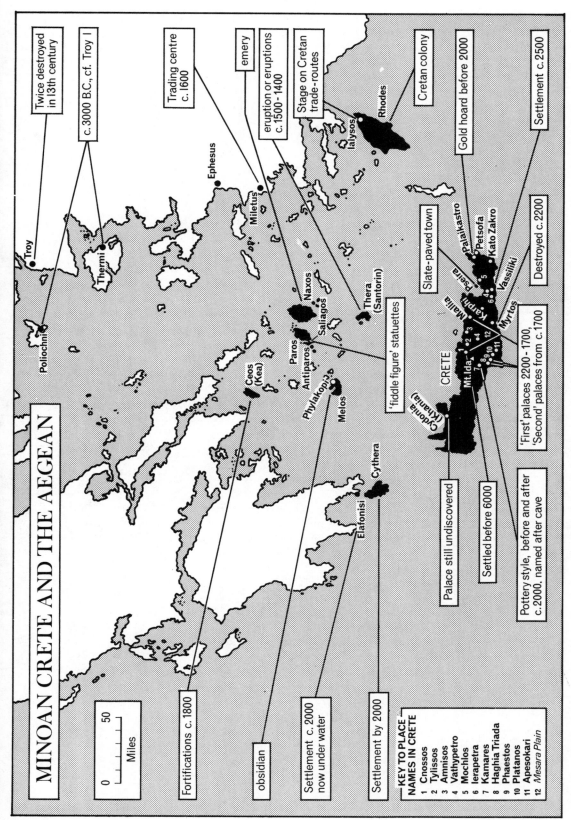

Twice destroyed in 13th century

c. 3000 B.C., cf. Troy I

Trading centre c. 1600

emery

eruption or eruptions c. 1500 - 1400

Stage on Cretan trade-routes

Cretan colony

Gold hoard before 2000

Settlement c. 2500

Destroyed c. 2200

Slate-paved town

'First' palaces 2200 - 1700, 'Second' palaces from c. 1700

Pottery style, before and after c. 2000, named after cave

Settled before 6000

Palace still undiscovered

Settlement by 2000

Settlement c. 2000 now under water

obsidian

Fortifications c. 1800

'fiddle figure' statuettes

Troy

Thermi

Poliochni

Ephesus

Miletus

Naxos

Saliagos

Paros

Antiparos

Ceos (Kea)

Phylakopi

Melos

Elafonisi

Cythera

Thera (Santorin)

Rhodes

Ialysos

CRETE

Cydonia (Khania)

Mt. Ida

Mallia

Karphi

Pseira

Palaikastro

Petsofa

Kato Zakro

Vassiliki

Myrtos

50

0

Miles

KEY TO PLACE NAMES IN CRETE

1 Cnossos
2 Tylissos
3 Amnisos
4 Vathypetro
5 Mochlos
6 Ierapetra
7 Kamares
8 Haghia Triada
9 Phaestos
10 Platanos
11 Apesokari
12 *Mesara Plain*

4

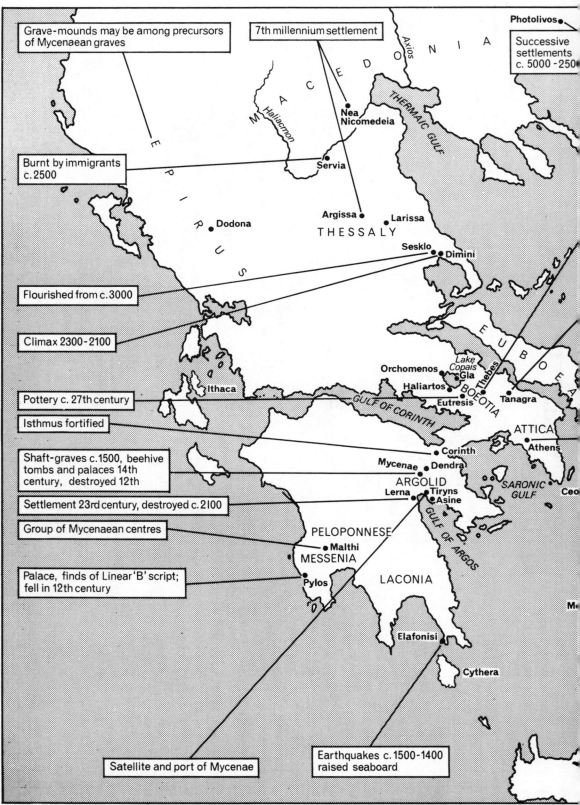

Grave-mounds may be among precursors of Mycenaean graves

7th millennium settlement

Successive settlements c. 5000 - 250

Burnt by immigrants c. 2500

Flourished from c. 3000

Climax 2300 - 2100

Pottery c. 27th century

Isthmus fortified

Shaft-graves c.1500, beehive tombs and palaces 14th century, destroyed 12th

Settlement 23rd century, destroyed c. 2100

Group of Mycenaean centres

Palace, finds of Linear 'B' script; fell in 12th century

Satellite and port of Mycenae

Earthquakes c. 1500-1400 raised seaboard

Photolivos

MACEDONIA

Axios

Haliacmon

Nea Nicomedeia

THERMAIC GULF

Servia

Argissa

Larissa

Dodona

THESSALY

Sesklo

Dimini

EPIRUS

Ithaca

EUBOEA

Lake Copais

Orchomenos

Gla

Thebes

Haliartos

BOEOTIA

Eutresis

Tanagra

GULF OF CORINTH

ATTICA

Athens

Corinth

Mycenae

Dendra

ARGOLID

Lerna

Tiryns

Asine

SARONIC GULF

Ceo

GULF OF ARGOS

PELOPONNESE

Malthi

MESSENIA

LACONIA

Pylos

M

Elafonisi

Cythera

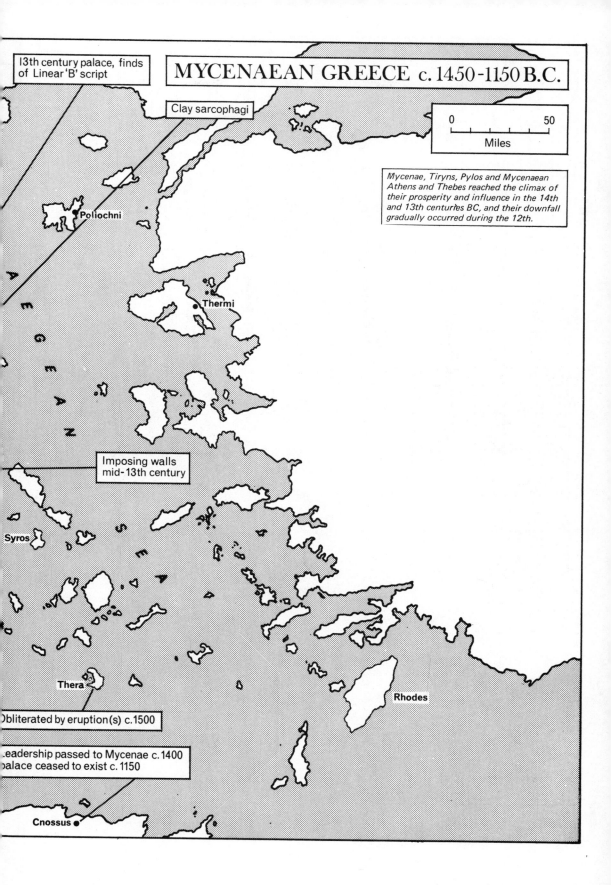

13th century palace, finds of Linear 'B' script

MYCENAEAN GREECE c. 1450-1150 B.C.

Clay sarcophagi

0   50

Miles

Mycenae, Tiryns, Pylos and Mycenaean Athens and Thebes reached the climax of their prosperity and influence in the 14th and 13th centuries BC, and their downfall gradually occurred during the 12th.

Poliochni

A
E
G
E
A
N

Thermi

Imposing walls mid-13th century

Syros

Thera

Rhodes

Obliterated by eruption(s) c.1500

Leadership passed to Mycenae c.1400 palace ceased to exist c.1150

Cnossus

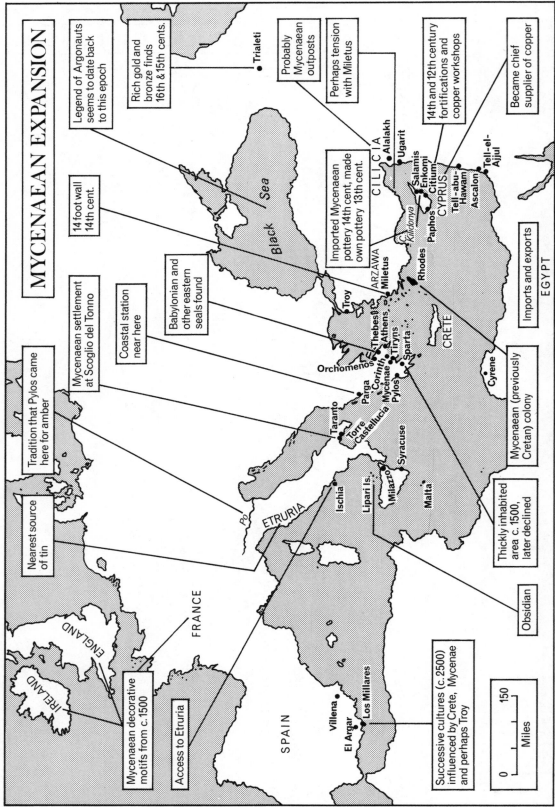

MYCENAEAN EXPANSION

Legend of Argonauts seems to date back to this epoch

Rich gold and bronze finds 16th & 15th cents.

Probably Mycenaean outposts

Perhaps tension with Miletus

14th and 12th century fortifications and copper workshops

Became chief supplier of copper

14 foot wall 14th cent.

Imported Mycenaean pottery 14th cent, made its own pottery 13th cent.

Mycenaean settlement at Scoglio del Tonno

Coastal station near here

Babylonian and other eastern seals found

Tradition that Pylos came here for amber

Nearest source of tin

Mycenaean decorative motifs from c.1500

Access to Etruria

Mycenaean (previously Cretan) colony

Thickly inhabited area c. 1500, later declined

Obsidian

Imports and exports

Successive cultures (c. 2500) influenced by Crete, Mycenae and perhaps Troy

Trialeti

Black Sea

CILICIA
Alalakh
• Ugarit
Salamis
Enkomi
Citium
CYPRUS
Tell-abu-Hawam
Ascalon
Tell-el-Ajjul
Paphos
Kition

EGYPT

ARZAWA
Miletus
Rhodes
CRETE
• Cyrene

Troy
Orchomenos
Thebes
Athens
Corinth
Mycenae
Tiryns
Sparta
Parga
Pylos

Taranto
Torre Castellucia
Syracuse
Milazzo
Lipari Is.
Malta
Ischia

Po
ETRURIA

FRANCE

ENGLAND
IRELAND

SPAIN
Villena
El Argar
Los Millares

0   150
Miles

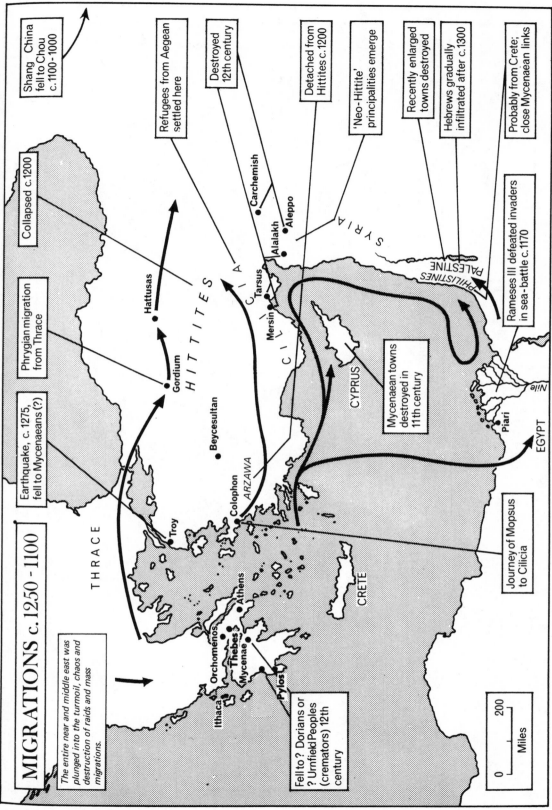

MIGRATIONS c. 1250 - 1100

The entire near and middle east was plunged into the turmoil, chaos and destruction of raids and mass migrations.

Shang China fell to Chou c. 1100-1000

Refugees from Aegean settled here

Destroyed 12th century

Detached from Hittites c. 1200

'Neo-Hittite' principalities emerge

Recently enlarged towns destroyed

Hebrews gradually infiltrated after c. 1300

Probably from Crete; close Mycenaean links

Rameses III defeated invaders in sea-battle c. 1170

Collapsed c. 1200

Phrygian migration from Thrace

Earthquake, c. 1275, fell to Mycenaeans (?)

Mycenaean towns destroyed in 11th century

Journey of Mopsus to Cilicia

Fell to? Dorians or ? Urnfield Peoples (cremators) 12th century

THRACE

Troy

Hattusas

Gordium

HITTITES

Beycesultan

Colophon

ARZAWA

Mersin

Tarsus

CILI

Alalakh

Carchemish

Aleppo

SYRIA

PALESTINE

PHILISTINES

Nile

Piari

EGYPT

CYPRUS

CRETE

Athens

Orchomenos

Thebes

Mycenae

Ithaca

Pylos

0   200

Miles

7

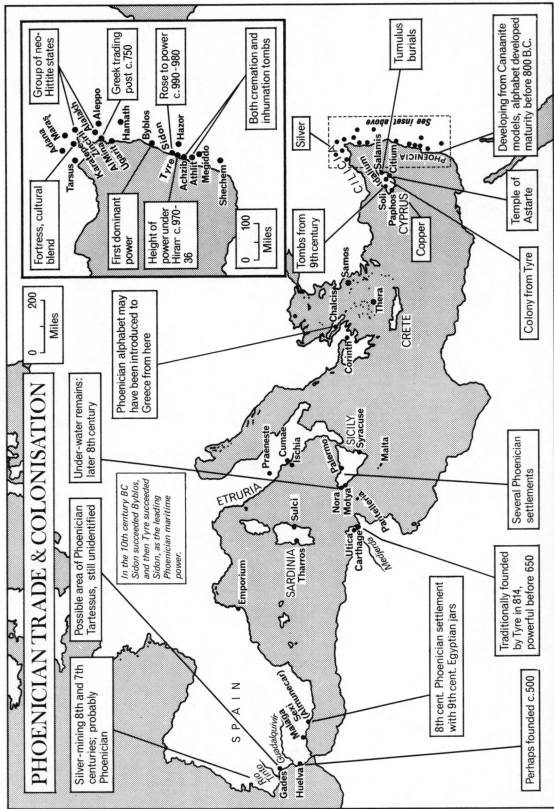

PHOENICIAN TRADE & COLONISATION

Silver-mining 8th and 7th centuries; probably Phoenician

Possible area of Phoenician Tartessus, still unidentified

Under-water remains: later 8th century

In the 10th century BC Sidon succeeded Byblos, and then Tyre succeeded Sidon, as the leading Phoenician maritime power.

Phoenician alphabet may have been introduced to Greece from here

0 — 200 Miles

Perhaps founded c.500

8th cent. Phoenician settlement with 9th cent. Egyptian jars

Traditionally founded by Tyre in 814, powerful before 650

Several Phoenician settlements

Colony from Tyre

S P A I N

Río Tinto
Guadalquivir
Gades
Huelva
Malaga
Sexi (Almuñecar)

Emporium
SARDINIA
Sulci
Tharros
Nora

ETRURIA

Praeneste
Cumae
Ischia

Palermo
Motya
Pantelleria
SICILY
Syracuse
Malta

Utica
Carthage
Mejierda

Chalcis
Corinth
Samos
Thera
CRETE

CYPRUS
Soli
Salamis
Paphos
Citium
Kition
CILICIA
PHOENICIA
See inset above

Copper
Silver
Tumulus burials
Temple of Astarte
Developing from Canaanite models, alphabet developed maturity before 800 B.C.

Inset

Group of neo-Hittite states

Greek trading post c.750

Rose to power c.990–980

Both cremation and inhumation tombs

Fortress, cultural blend

First dominant power

Height of power under Hiram c.970–36

Tombs from 9th century

Apana
Alvara
Aleppo
Tarsus
Karatepe
Al Mina
Alalakh
Ugarit
Hamath
Byblos
Sidon
Tyre
Achzib
Athlit
Megiddo
Hazor
Shechem

0 — 100 Miles

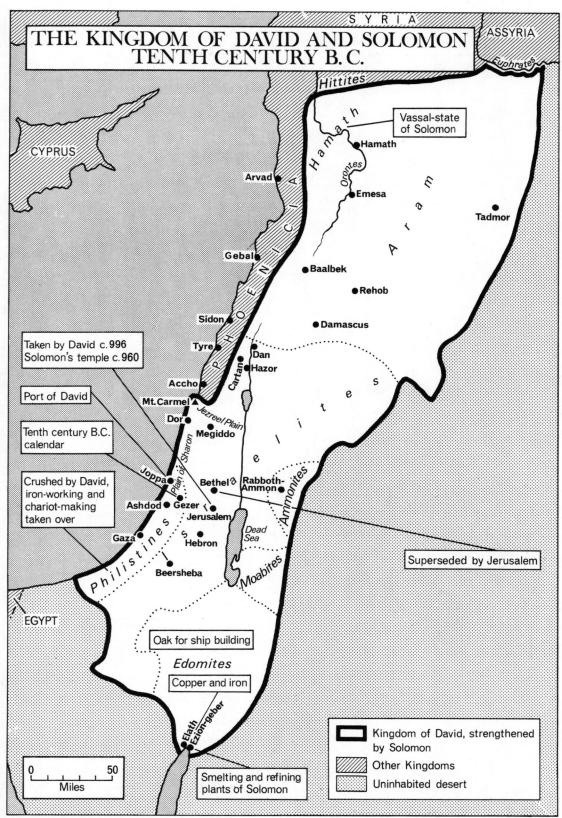

THE KINGDOM OF DAVID AND SOLOMON TENTH CENTURY B.C.

SYRIA

ASSYRIA

Euphrates

Hittites

CYPRUS

Vassal-state of Solomon

Hamath

Arvad

Orontes

Emesa

Aram

Tadmor

Gebal

Baalbek

Rehob

Sidon

Damascus

Taken by David c.996
Solomon's temple c.960

Tyre

Dan

Hazor

Cartan

Port of David

Accho

Israelites

Mt. Carmel

Tenth century B.C. calendar

Dor

Jezreel Plain

Megiddo

Crushed by David, iron-working and chariot-making taken over

Joppa

Plain of Sharon

Bethel

Rabboth-Ammon

Ammonites

Ashdod

Gezer

Jerusalem

Gaza

Hebron

Dead Sea

Superseded by Jerusalem

Philistines

Beersheba

Moabites

EGYPT

Oak for ship building

Edomites

Copper and iron

Elath
Ezion-geber

0   50
Miles

Smelting and refining plants of Solomon

	Kingdom of David, strengthened by Solomon
	Other Kingdoms
	Uninhabited desert

9

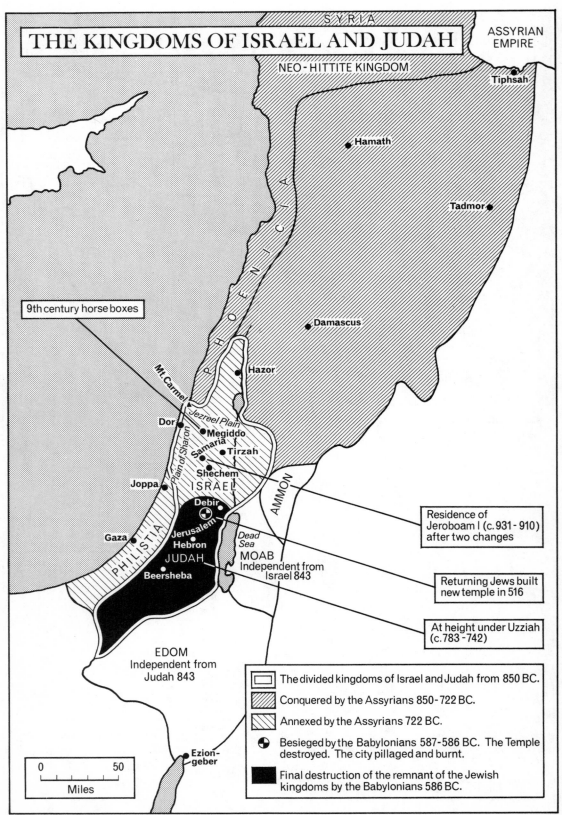

THE KINGDOMS OF ISRAEL AND JUDAH

SYRIA

ASSYRIAN EMPIRE

NEO-HITTITE KINGDOM

Tiphsah

Hamath

Tadmor

9th century horse boxes

Damascus

P H O E N I C I A

Mt Carmel

Hazor

Dor

Jezreel Plain

Megiddo

Samaria

Tirzah

Plain of Sharon

Shechem

Joppa

ISRAEL

AMMON

Residence of Jeroboam I (c.931-910) after two changes

Debir

Gaza

Jerusalem

Dead Sea

Hebron

MOAB
Independent from Israel 843

Returning Jews built new temple in 516

PHILISTIA

JUDAH

Beersheba

At height under Uzziah (c.783-742)

EDOM
Independent from Judah 843

Ezion-geber

The divided kingdoms of Israel and Judah from 850 BC.

Conquered by the Assyrians 850-722 BC.

Annexed by the Assyrians 722 BC.

Besieged by the Babylonians 587-586 BC. The Temple destroyed. The city pillaged and burnt.

Final destruction of the remnant of the Jewish kingdoms by the Babylonians 586 BC.

0   50
Miles

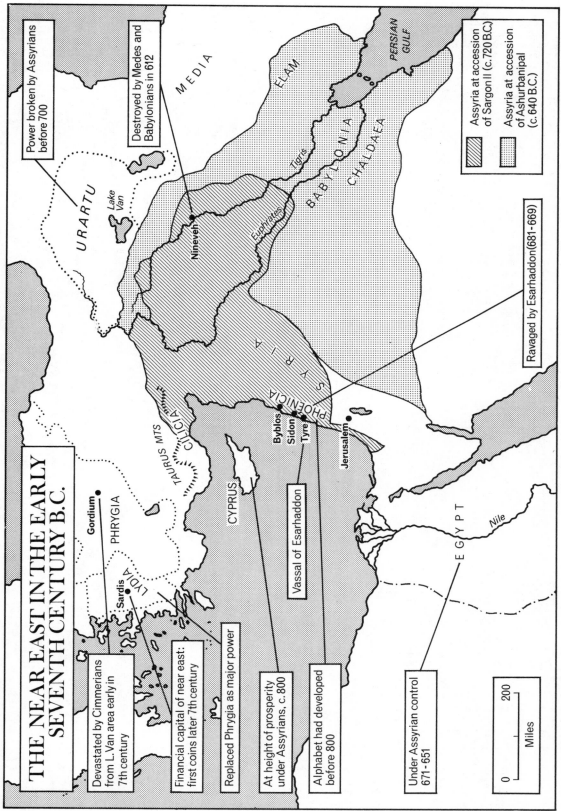

THE NEAR EAST IN THE EARLY SEVENTH CENTURY B.C.

Power broken by Assyrians before 700

Destroyed by Medes and Babylonians in 612

Assyria at accession of Sargon II (c. 720 B.C.)

Assyria at accession of Ashurbanipal (c. 640 B.C.)

Ravaged by Esarhaddon (681-669)

Devastated by Cimmerians from L. Van area early in 7th century

Financial capital of near east: first coins later 7th century

Replaced Phrygia as major power

Vassal of Esarhaddon

At height of prosperity under Assyrians, c. 800

Alphabet had developed before 800

Under Assyrian control 671 - 651

MEDIA

ELAM

PERSIAN GULF

BABYLONIA

CHALDAEA

URARTU

Lake Van

Nineveh

Euphrates

Tigris

SYRIA

TAURUS MTS

CILICIA

PHOENICIA

Byblos

Sidon

Tyre

Jerusalem

CYPRUS

Gordium

PHRYGIA

Sardis

LYDIA

EGYPT

Nile

0   200

Miles

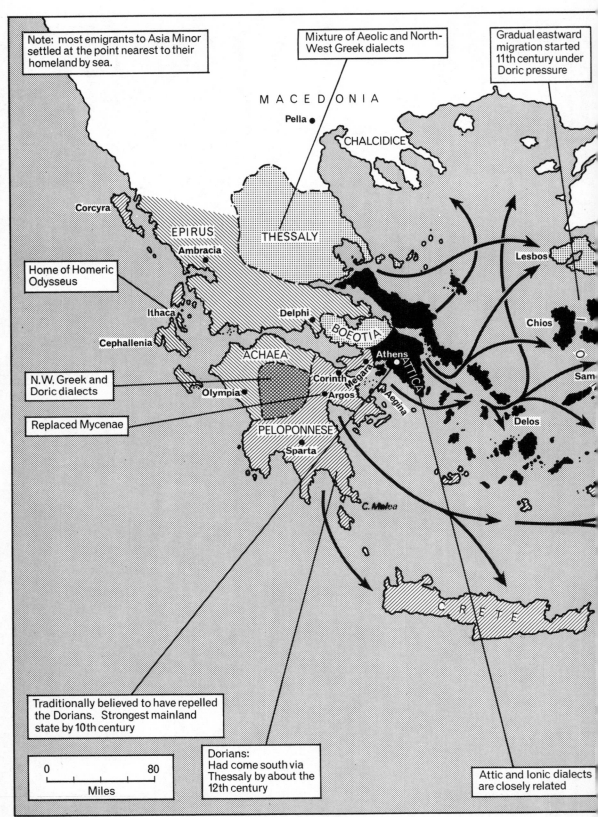

Note: most emigrants to Asia Minor settled at the point nearest to their homeland by sea.

Mixture of Aeolic and North-West Greek dialects

Gradual eastward migration started 11th century under Doric pressure

MACEDONIA

Pella ●

CHALCIDICE

EPIRUS

Corcyra

THESSALY

Ambracia ●

Home of Homeric Odysseus

Ithaca ●

Delphi ●

BOEOTIA

Cephallenia

ACHAEA

Athens ●

ATTICA

Lesbos

Chios

N.W. Greek and Doric dialects

Olympia ●

Corinth

Megara

Argos ●

Aegina ●

Sam

Replaced Mycenae

PELOPONNESE

Delos

Sparta ●

C. Malea

CRETE

Traditionally believed to have repelled the Dorians. Strongest mainland state by 10th century

Dorians: Had come south via Thessaly by about the 12th century

Attic and Ionic dialects are closely related

0   80

Miles

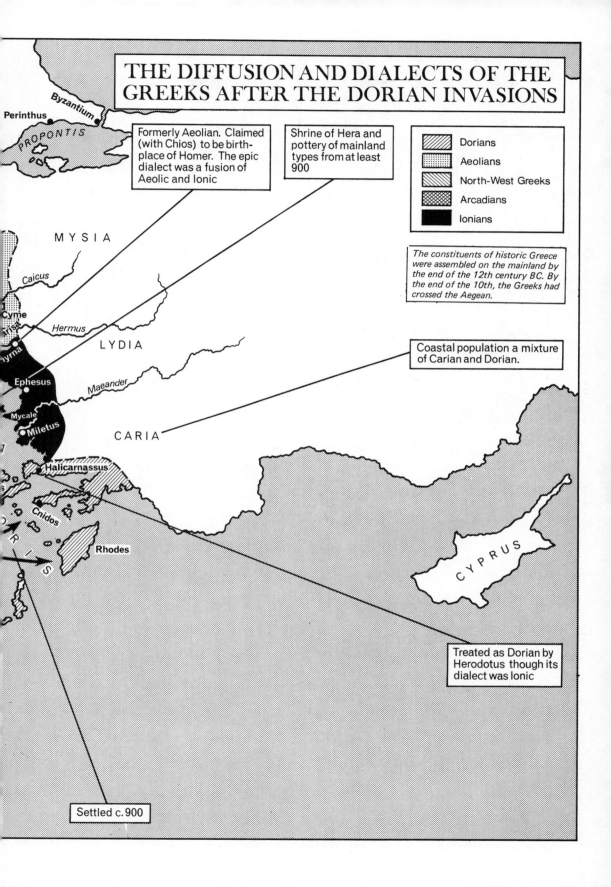

THE DIFFUSION AND DIALECTS OF THE GREEKS AFTER THE DORIAN INVASIONS

Byzantium

Perinthus

PROPONTIS

Formerly Aeolian. Claimed (with Chios) to be birth-place of Homer. The epic dialect was a fusion of Aeolic and Ionic

Shrine of Hera and pottery of mainland types from at least 900

Dorians

Aeolians

North-West Greeks

Arcadians

Ionians

The constituents of historic Greece were assembled on the mainland by the end of the 12th century BC. By the end of the 10th, the Greeks had crossed the Aegean.

MYSIA

Caicus

Cyme

Hermus

LYDIA

Coastal population a mixture of Carian and Dorian.

Ephesus

Maeander

Mycale

Miletus

CARIA

Halicarnassus

D O R I S

Cnidos

Rhodes

CYPRUS

Treated as Dorian by Herodotus though its dialect was Ionic

Settled c. 900

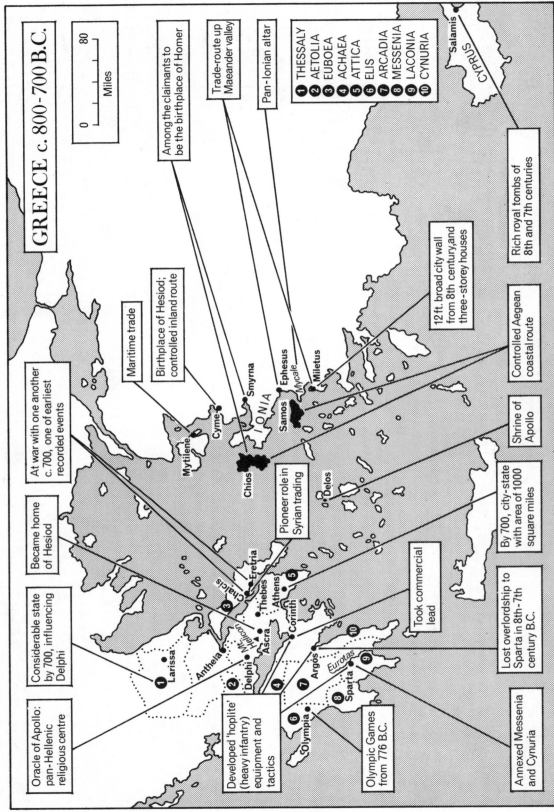

GREECE c. 800-700 B.C.

Miles
0 ——— 80

1 THESSALY
2 AETOLIA
3 EUBOEA
4 ACHAEA
5 ATTICA
6 ELIS
7 ARCADIA
8 MESSENIA
9 LACONIA
10 CYNURIA

Among the claimants to be the birthplace of Homer

Trade-route up Maeander valley

Pan-Ionian altar

Rich royal tombs of 8th and 7th centuries

Maritime trade

Birthplace of Hesiod; controlled inland route

12 ft. broad city wall from 8th century, and three-storey houses

Controlled Aegean coastal route

At war with one another c. 700, one of earliest recorded events

Pioneer role in Syrian trading

Shrine of Apollo

Became home of Hesiod

By 700, city-state with area of 1000 square miles

Considerable state by 700, influencing Delphi

Took commercial lead

Lost overlordship to Sparta in 8th-7th century B.C.

Oracle of Apollo: pan-Hellenic religious centre

Developed 'hoplite' (heavy infantry) equipment and tactics

Olympic Games from 776 B.C.

Annexed Messenia and Cynuria

IONIA

Salamis
CYPRUS

Smyrna
Cyme
Mytilene
Chios
Samos
Ephesus
Mycale
Miletus
Delos

Eretria
Chalcis
Thebes
Athens
Corinth
Ascra
Helicon
Delphi
Anthela
Larissa
Argos
Eurotas
Sparta
Olympia

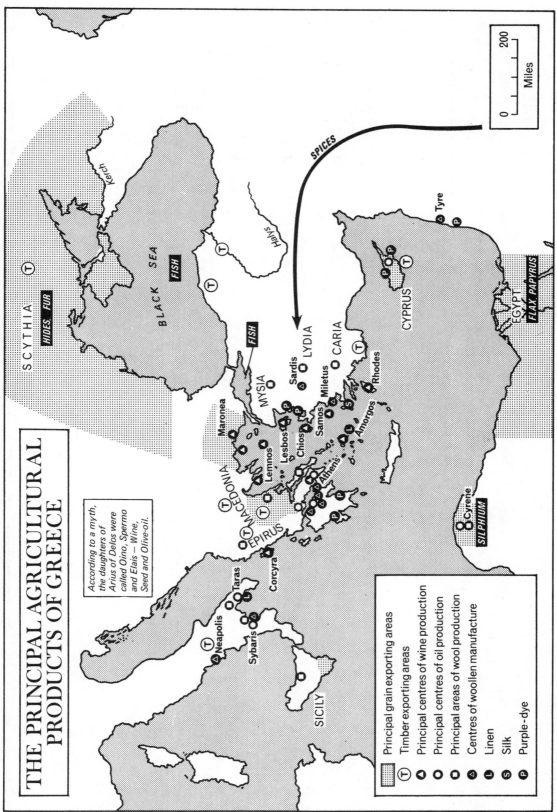

THE PRINCIPAL AGRICULTURAL PRODUCTS OF GREECE

According to a myth, the daughters of Arius of Delos were called Oino, Spermo and Elais – Wine, Seed and Olive-oil.

▦	Principal grain exporting areas
Ⓣ	Timber exporting areas
◢	Principal centres of wine production
◯	Principal centres of oil production
⬠	Principal areas of wool production
◮	Centres of woollen manufacture
Ⓛ	Linen
Ⓢ	Silk
Ⓟ	Purple-dye

SCYTHIA

HIDES   FUR

BLACK SEA

FISH

Kerch

Halys

SPICES

200

0

Miles

Tyre

CYPRUS

EGYPT

FLAX PAPYRUS

FISH

Sardis   LYDIA

CARIA

MYSIA

Maronea

Lesbos   Chios

Samos Miletus

Rhodes

Amorgos

Athens

Lemnos

MACEDONIA

EPIRUS

Corcyra

Taras

Neapolis

Sybaris

SICILY

Cyrene

SILPHIUM

14

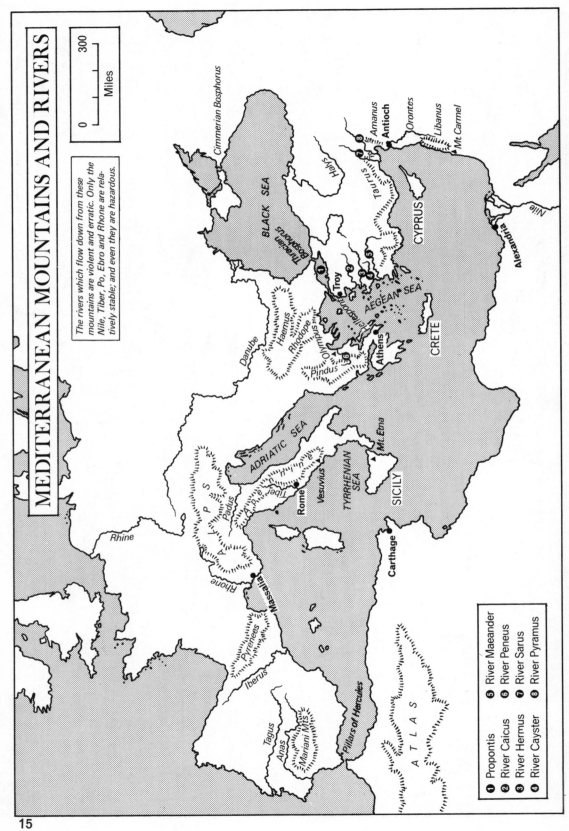

MEDITERRANEAN MOUNTAINS AND RIVERS

The rivers which flow down from these mountains are violent and erratic. Only the Nile, Tiber, Po, Ebro and Rhone are relatively stable, and even they are hazardous.

0 — 300

Miles

Rivers

1. Propontis
2. River Caicus
3. River Hermus
4. River Cayster
5. River Maeander
6. River Peneus
7. River Sarus
8. River Pyramus

Cimmerian Bosphorus

BLACK SEA

Thracian Bosphorus

Danube

Haemus

Rhodope

Pindus

Olympus

Troy

Thessalia

AEGEAN SEA

Athens

CRETE

Halys

Taurus

Amanus
Antioch
Orontes
Libanus
Mt Carmel

CYPRUS

Nile

Alexandria

ALPS

Padus

Apennines

Tiber

Rome

Vesuvius

Mt. Etna

ADRIATIC SEA

TYRRHENIAN SEA

SICILY

Carthage

Massalia

Rhone

Pyrenees

Iberus

Rhine

Tagus

Anas

Mariani Mts

Pillars of Hercules

ATLAS

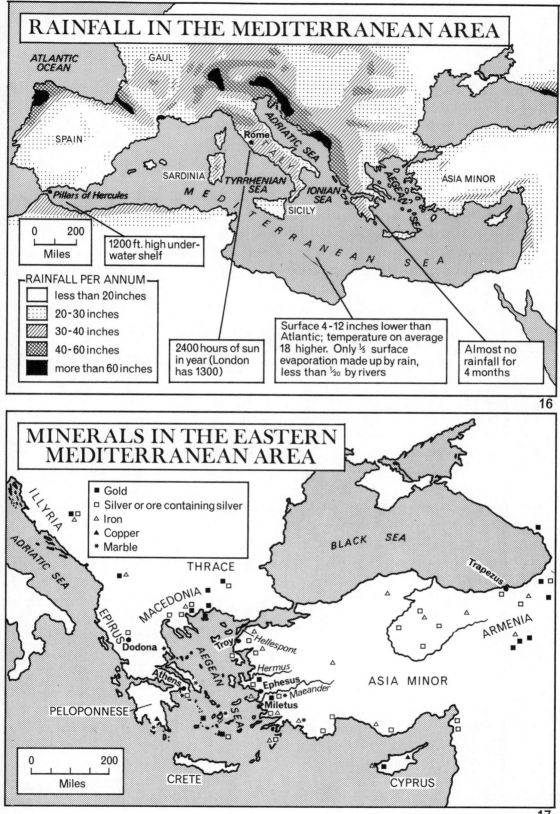

RAINFALL IN THE MEDITERRANEAN AREA

ATLANTIC OCEAN

GAUL

SPAIN

Rome

SARDINIA

TYRRHENIAN SEA

ITALY

ADRIATIC SEA

IONIAN SEA

SICILY

M E D I T E R R A N E A N   S E A

AEGEAN SEA

ASIA MINOR

Pillars of Hercules

0   200
Miles

1200 ft. high under-water shelf

RAINFALL PER ANNUM

- less than 20 inches
- 20-30 inches
- 30-40 inches
- 40-60 inches
- more than 60 inches

2400 hours of sun in year (London has 1300)

Surface 4-12 inches lower than Atlantic; temperature on average 18 higher. Only ⅓ surface evaporation made up by rain, less than ¹⁄₂₀ by rivers

Almost no rainfall for 4 months

MINERALS IN THE EASTERN MEDITERRANEAN AREA

- ■ Gold
- □ Silver or ore containing silver
- △ Iron
- ▲ Copper
- ＊ Marble

ILLYRIA

ADRIATIC SEA

THRACE

BLACK SEA

Trapezus

MACEDONIA

EPIRUS

Dodona

Troy

Hellespont

Hermus

AEGEAN SEA

Athens

Ephesus

Maeander

Miletus

ARMENIA

ASIA MINOR

PELOPONNESE

0   200
Miles

CRETE

CYPRUS

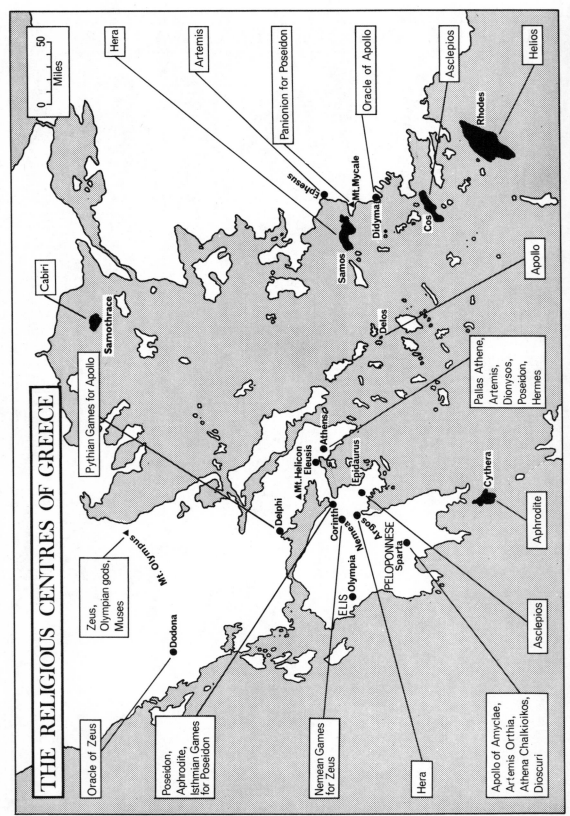

THE RELIGIOUS CENTRES OF GREECE

Oracle of Zeus

Zeus, Olympian gods, Muses

Poseidon, Aphrodite, Isthmian Games for Poseidon

Pythian Games for Apollo

Cabiri

Hera

Artemis

Panionion for Poseidon

Oracle of Apollo

Asclepios

Helios

Apollo

Pallas Athene, Artemis, Dionysos, Poseidon, Hermes

Nemean Games for Zeus

Hera

Apollo of Amyclae, Artemis Orthia, Athena Chalkioikos, Dioscuri

Asclepios

Aphrodite

50 Miles

Dodona

Mt. Olympus

Delphi

Mt. Helicon

Eleusis

Athens

Epidaurus

Corinth

Nemea

Argos

ELIS

Olympia

PELOPONNESE

Sparta

Cythera

Samothrace

Ephesus

Mt. Mycale

Didyma

Cos

Samos

Rhodes

Delos

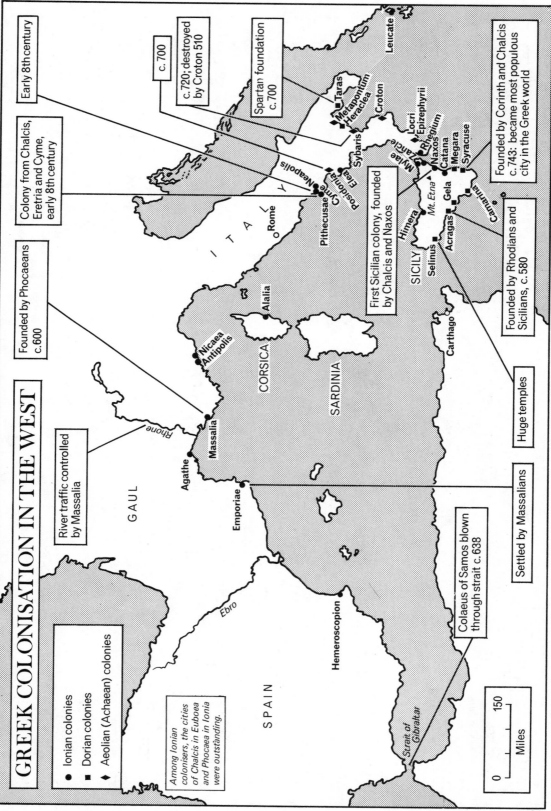

GREEK COLONISATION IN THE WEST

- ● Ionian colonies
- ■ Dorian colonies
- ◆ Aeolian (Achaean) colonies

Among Ionian colonisers, the cities of Chalcis in Euboea and Phocaea in Ionia were outstanding.

Early 8th century

Colony from Chalcis, Eretria and Cyme, early 8th century

c. 700

c.720; destroyed by Croton 510

Spartan foundation c. 700

Founded by Corinth and Chalcis c.743: became most populous city in the Greek world

Founded by Phocaeans c.600

First Sicilian colony, founded by Chalcis and Naxos

Founded by Rhodians and Sicilians, c. 580

River traffic controlled by Massalia

Huge temples

Settled by Massalians

Colaeus of Samos blown through strait c. 638

Leucate

Taras
Metapontum
Heraclea
Croton

Locri
Epizephyrii
Rhegium
Zancle
Myiae
Naxos
Catana
Megara
Syracuse

Sybaris
Elea
Posidonia
Neapolis
Cyme
Pithecusae

Rome

SICILY
Mt. Etna
Himera
Selinus
Acragas
Gela
Camarina

Carthago

ITALY

Alalia

CORSICA

SARDINIA

Nicaea
Antipolis

Massalia
Agathe
Rhone

GAUL

Emporiae

Ebro

Hemeroscopion

SPAIN

Strait of Gibraltar

0   150
Miles

19

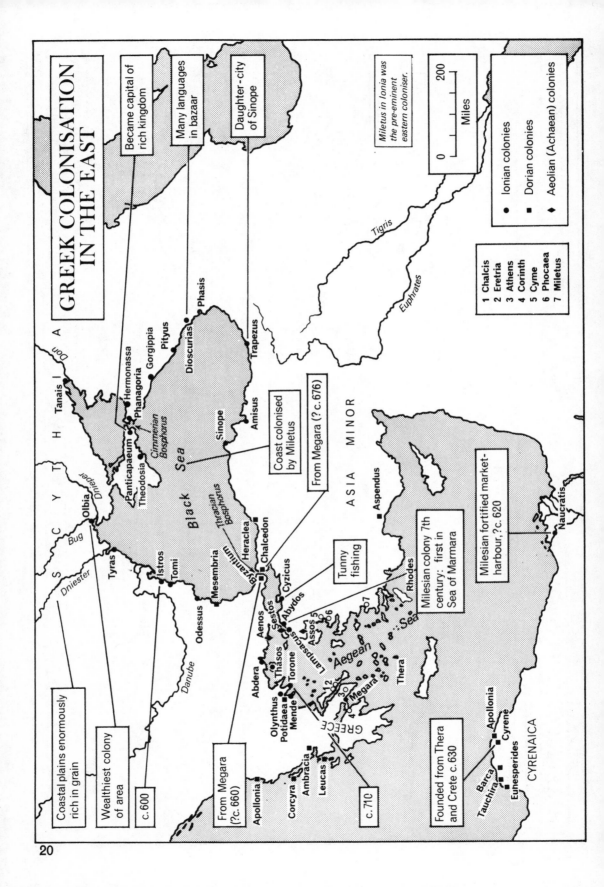

GREEK COLONISATION IN THE EAST

Miletus in Ionia was the pre-eminent eastern coloniser.

0   200

Miles

● Ionian colonies
■ Dorian colonies
◆ Aeolian (Achaean) colonies

1 Chalcis
2 Eretria
3 Athens
4 Corinth
5 Cyme
6 Phocaea
7 Miletus

Became capital of rich kingdom

Many languages in bazaar

Daughter-city of Sinope

Coast colonised by Miletus

From Megara (? c. 676)

Tunny fishing

Milesian colony 7th century: first in Sea of Marmara

Milesian fortified market-harbour, ? c. 620

Coastal plains enormously rich in grain

Wealthiest colony of area

c. 600

From Megara (? c. 660)

c. 710

Founded from Thera and Crete c. 630

Place names

Tigris

Euphrates

Don

A

Tanais

S C Y T H I A

Dnieper

Bug

Olbia

Tyras

Dniester

Istros

Tomi

Mesembria

Odessus

Danube

Phasis

Dioscurias

Pityus

Gorgippia

Hermonassa

Phanagoria

Cimmerian Bosphorus

Panticapaeum

Theodosia

Black Sea

Sinope

Amisus

Trapezus

Thracian Bosphorus

Heraclea

Chalcedon

Byzantium

Cyzicus

Abydos

Sestos

Aenos

Lampsacus

Abdera

Thásos

Torone

Olynthus

Potidaea

Mende

Megara

GREECE

Apollonia

Corcyra

Ambracia

Leucas

Assos

Aegean Sea

Rhodes

Thera

ASIA MINOR

Aspendus

Naucratis

Apollonia

Cyrene

Barca

Tauchira

Eunesperides

CYRENAICA

20

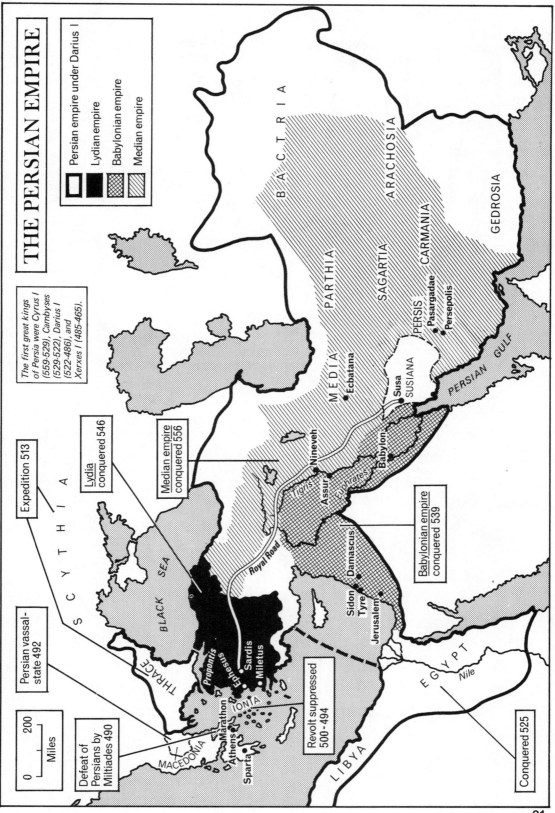

THE PERSIAN EMPIRE

Persian empire under Darius I
Lydian empire
Babylonian empire
Median empire

The first great kings of Persia were Cyrus I (559-529), Cambyses (529-522), Darius I (522-486), and Xerxes I (485-465).

Expedition 513

Lydia conquered 546

Median empire conquered 556

Babylonian empire conquered 539

Persian vassal-state 492

Revolt suppressed 500-494

Defeat of Persians by Miltiades 490

Conquered 525

0   200
Miles

BACTRIA

ARACHOSIA

GEDROSIA

PARTHIA

SAGARTIA

CARMANIA

PERSIS

Pasargadae
Persepolis

MEDIA

Ecbatana

Susa
SUSIANA

PERSIAN GULF

Nineveh

Assur

Tigris
Euphrates

Babylon

Royal Road

Damascus
Sidon
Tyre
Jerusalem

EGYPT
Nile

LIBYA

SCYTHIA

THRACE

BLACK SEA

Propontis
Ephesus
Sardis
Miletus
IONIA

Marathon
Athens
Sparta

MACEDONIA

21

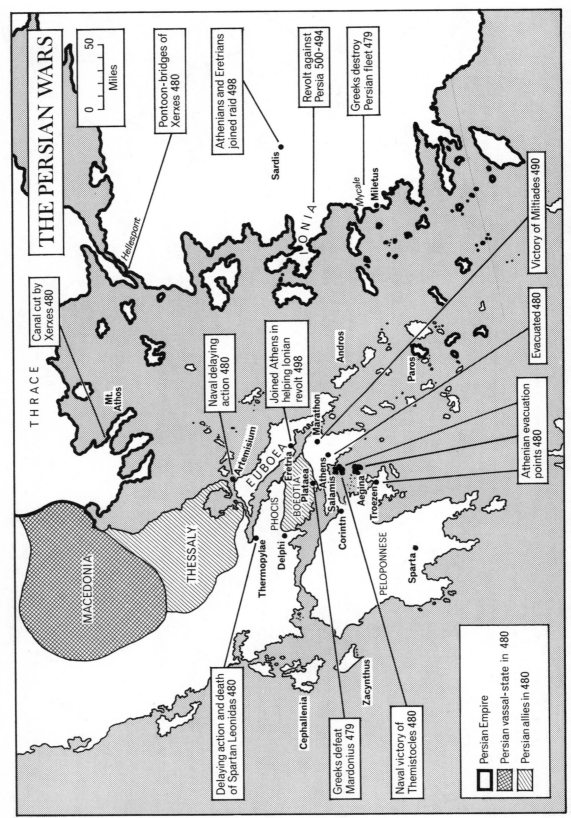

THE PERSIAN WARS

Pontoon-bridges of Xerxes 480

Athenians and Eretrians joined raid 498

Revolt against Persia 500–494

Greeks destroy Persian fleet 479

Canal cut by Xerxes 480

Naval delaying action 480

Joined Athens in helping Ionian revolt 498

Victory of Miltiades 490

Evacuated 480

Athenian evacuation points 480

Delaying action and death of Spartan Leonidas 480

Greeks defeat Mardonius 479

Naval victory of Themistocles 480

THRACE

MACEDONIA

THESSALY

PHOCIS

BOEOTIA

EUBOEA

IONIA

PELOPONNESE

Hellespont

Mt. Athos

Sardis

Mycale

Miletus

Andros

Paros

Artemisium

Thermopylae

Delphi

Eretria

Plataea

Marathon

Athens

Salamis

Aegina

Troezen

Corinth

Sparta

Cephallenia

Zacynthus

Miles
0   50

Persian Empire

Persian vassal-state in 480

Persian allies in 480

22

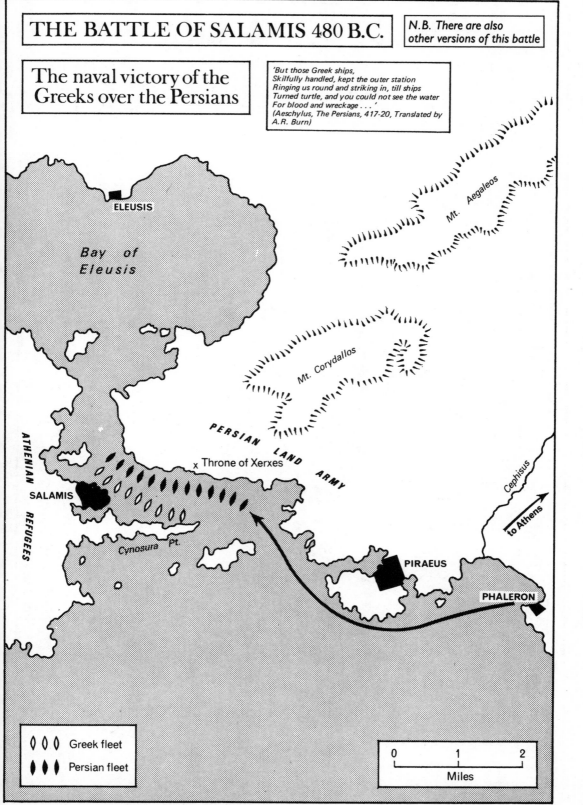

THE BATTLE OF SALAMIS 480 B.C.

N.B. There are also other versions of this battle

The naval victory of the Greeks over the Persians

'But those Greek ships,
Skilfully handled, kept the outer station
Ringing us round and striking in, till ships
Turned turtle, and you could not see the water
For blood and wreckage . . . '
(Aeschylus, The Persians, 417-20, Translated by
A.R. Burn)

ELEUSIS

Bay of
Eleusis

Mt. Aegaleos

Mt. Corydallos

PERSIAN LAND ARMY

x Throne of Xerxes

SALAMIS

ATHENIAN REFUGEES

Cynosura Pt.

Cephisus

to Athens

PIRAEUS

PHALERON

◊ ◊ ◊ Greek fleet

◆ ◆ ◆ Persian fleet

0   1   2
Miles

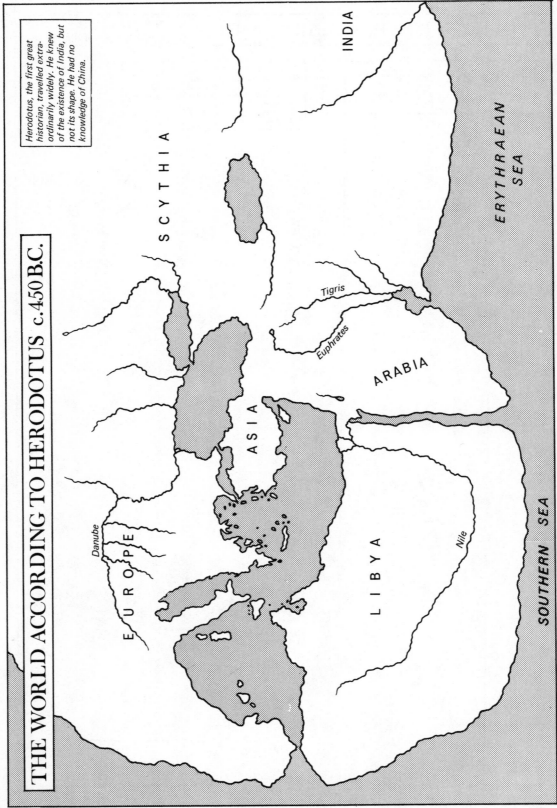

THE WORLD ACCORDING TO HERODOTUS c.450 B.C.

Herodotus, the first great historian, travelled extraordinarily widely. He knew of the existence of India, but not its shape. He had no knowledge of China.

SCYTHIA

INDIA

ERYTHRAEAN SEA

Tigris

Euphrates

ARABIA

ASIA

EUROPE

Danube

LIBYA

Nile

SOUTHERN SEA

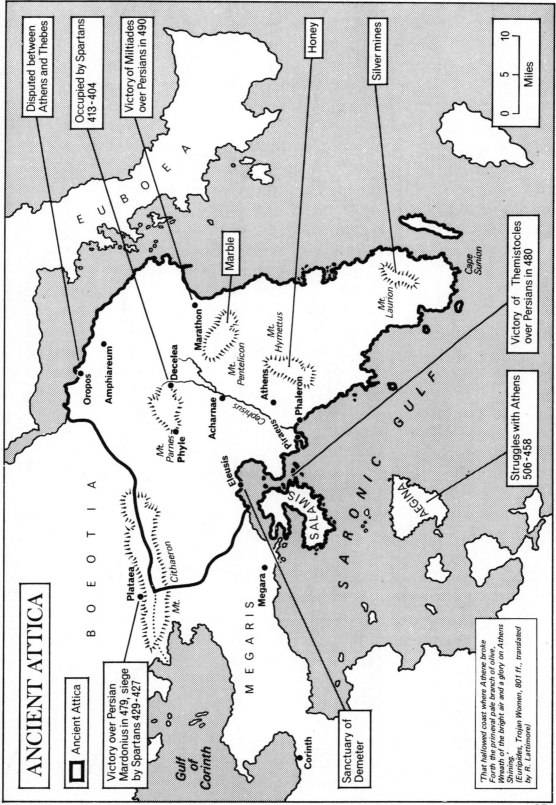

ANCIENT ATTICA

☐ Ancient Attica

Disputed between Athens and Thebes

Occupied by Spartans 413-404

Victory of Miltiades over Persians in 490

Honey

Silver mines

Marble

Victory over Persian Mardonius in 479, siege by Spartans 429-427

Victory of Themistocles over Persians in 480

Struggles with Athens 506-458

Sanctuary of Demeter

EUBOEA

BOEOTIA

MEGARIS

Gulf of Corinth

SARONIC GULF

SALAMIS

AEGINA

Cape Sunion

Corinth

Megara

Plataea

Mt. Cithaeron

Mt. Parnes

Phyle

Eleusis

Acharnae

Oropos

Amphiareum

Decelea

Marathon

Mt. Pentelicon

Athens

Phaleron

Piraeus

Cephisus

Mt. Hymettus

Mt. Laurion

'That hallowed coast where Athene broke
Forth the primeval pale branch of olive,
Wreath the bright air and a glory on Athens
Shining.'
(Euripides, Trojan Women, 801 ff., translated
by R. Lattimore)

0   5   10
Miles

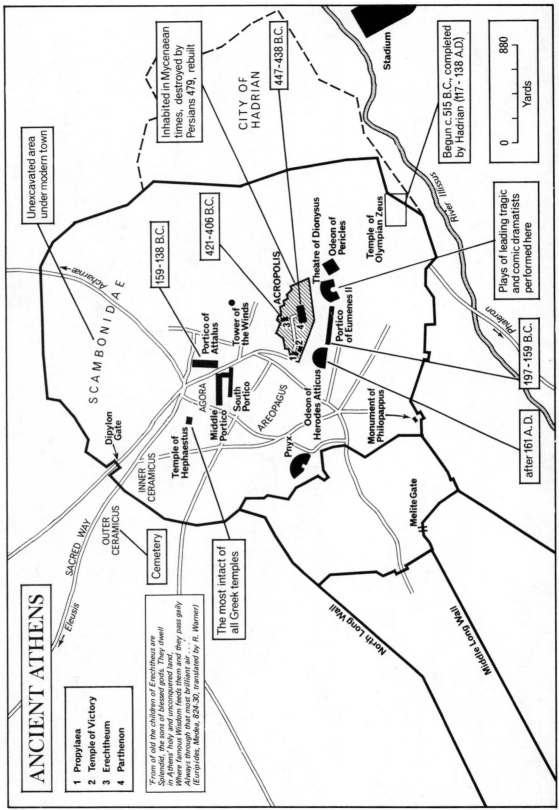

ANCIENT ATHENS

1 Propylaea
2 Temple of Victory
3 Erechtheum
4 Parthenon

"From of old the children of Erechtheus are
Splendid, the sons of blessed gods. They dwell
in Athens' holy and unconquered land,
Where famous Wisdom feeds them and they pass gaily
Always through that most brilliant air . . .'
(Euripides, Medea, 824-30, translated by R. Warner)

Cemetery

The most intact of
all Greek temples

Inhabited in Mycenaean
times, destroyed by
Persians 479, rebuilt

447-438 B.C.

159-138 B.C.

421-406 B.C.

CITY OF HADRIAN

Plays of leading tragic
and comic dramatists
performed here

Begun c.515 B.C., completed
by Hadrian (117 - 138 A.D.)

197-159 B.C.

after 161 A.D.

Unexcavated area
under modern town

880

0   Yards

Stadium

River Illissus

Phaleron

Achariae

SCAMBONIDAE

Dipylon
Gate

SACRED WAY

Eleusis

OUTER
CERAMICUS

INNER
CERAMICUS

Temple of
Hephaestus

AGORA

Middle
Portico

South
Portico

Portico of
Attalus

Tower of
the Winds

ACROPOLIS

1 3
2 4

Theatre of Dionysus

Odeon of
Pericles

Temple of
Olympian Zeus

Portico
of Eumenes II

Odeon of
Herodes Atticus

AREOPAGUS

Pnyx

Monument of
Philopappus

Melite Gate

North Long Wall

Middle Long Wall

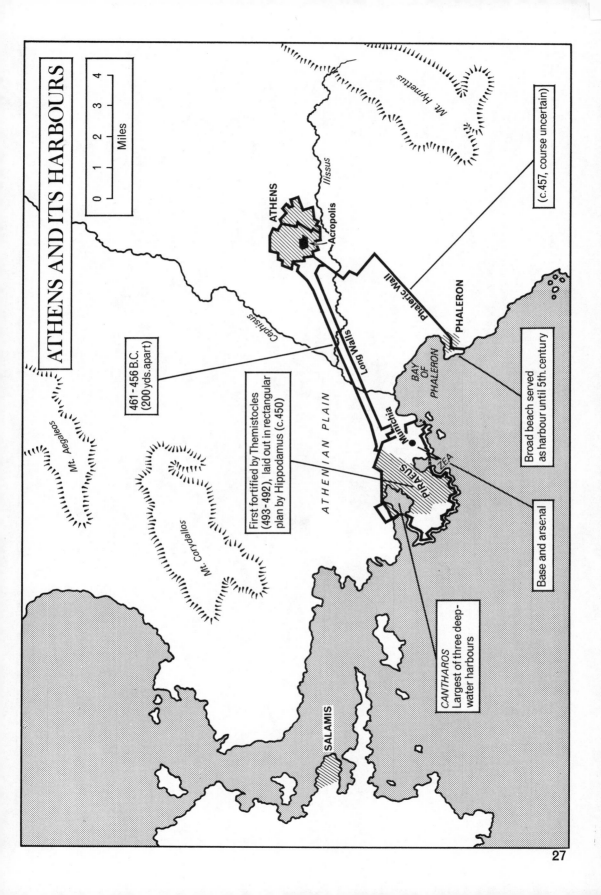

ATHENS AND ITS HARBOURS

Miles
0 1 2 3 4

Mt. Aegaleos

Mt. Corydallos

SALAMIS

ATHENIAN PLAIN

Mt. Hymettus

ATHENS

Acropolis

Ilissus

Cephisus

Long Walls

Phaleric Wall

(c.457, course uncertain)

PHALERON

BAY OF PHALERON

Munichia

ZEA

PIRAEUS

461 - 456 B.C. (200 yds. apart)

First fortified by Themistocles (493-492), laid out in rectangular plan by Hippodamus (c.450)

CANTHAROS
Largest of three deep-water harbours

Base and arsenal

Broad beach served as harbour until 5th. century

27

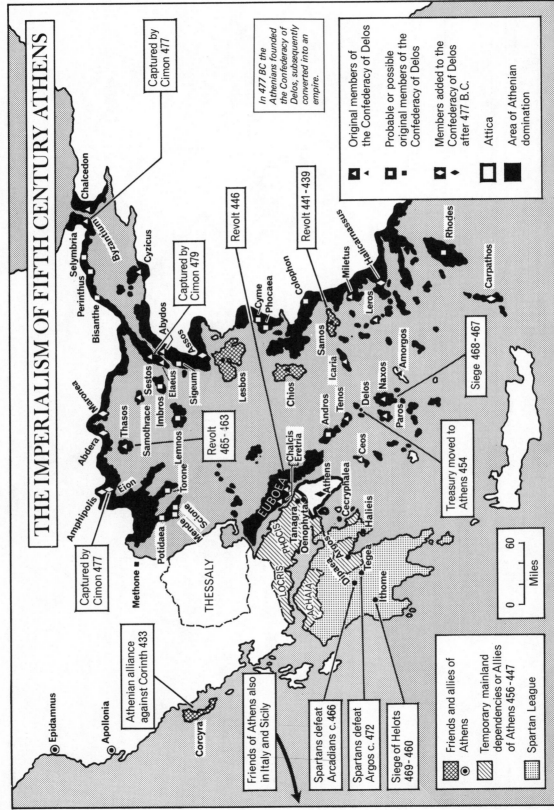

THE IMPERIALISM OF FIFTH CENTURY ATHENS

In 477 BC the Athenians founded the Confederacy of Delos, subsequently converted into an empire.

Original members of the Confederacy of Delos

Probable or possible original members of the Confederacy of Delos

Members added to the Confederacy of Delos after 477 B.C.

Attica

Area of Athenian domination

Captured by Cimon 477

Chalcedon

Byzantium

Perinthus

Selymbria

Bisanthe

Cyzicus

Captured by Cimon 479

Abydos

Assos

Sigeum

Elaeus

Imbros

Lemnos

Sestos

Samothrace

Thasos

Abdera

Maronea

Eion

Amphipolis

Captured by Cimon 477

Methone

Torone

Scione

Mende

Potidaea

THESSALY

Revolt 465-463

Chalcis

Eretria

Tanagra

Oenophyta

LOCRIS

PHOCIS

Athens

EUBOEA

Ceos

Cecryphalea

Halieis

Aegina

Dipaea

Tegea

ACHAIA

Ithome

Revolt 446

Cyme

Phocaea

Colophon

Miletus

Halicarnassus

Revolt 441-439

Rhodes

Carpathos

Lesbos

Chios

Samos

Icaria

Leros

Amorgos

Andros

Tenos

Delos

Naxos

Paros

Siege 468-467

Treasury moved to Athens 454

Friends of Athens also as in Italy and Sicily

Athenian alliance against Corinth 433

Corcyra

Apollonia

Epidamnus

Spartans defeat Arcadians c.466

Spartans defeat Argos c.472

Siege of Helots 469-460

Friends and allies of Athens

Temporary mainland dependencies or Allies of Athens 456-447

Spartan League

0   60

Miles

28

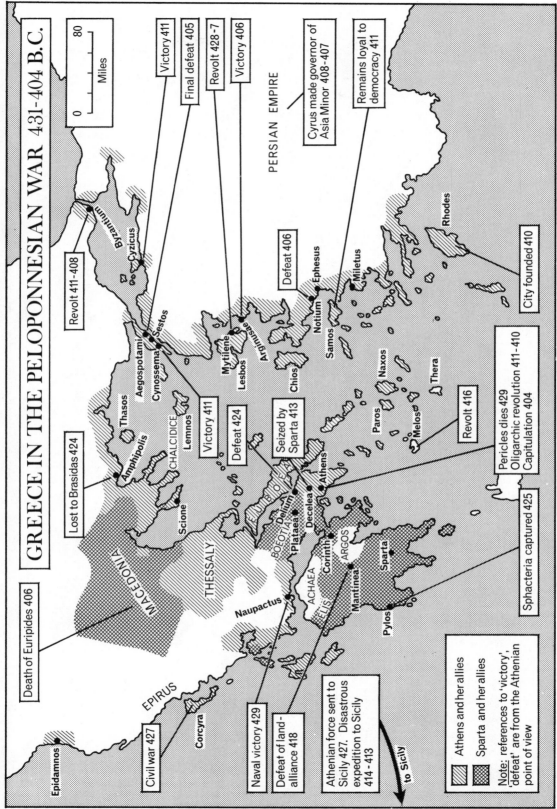

GREECE IN THE PELOPONNESIAN WAR 431–404 B.C.

0   80

Miles

Victory 411

Final defeat 405

Revolt 428-7

Victory 406

Cyrus made governor of Asia Minor 408-407

Remains loyal to democracy 411

PERSIAN EMPIRE

Revolt 411–408

Lost to Brasidas 424

Death of Euripides 406

Byzantium

Cyzicus

Sestos

Aegospotami

Cynossema

Thasos

Amphipolis

CHALCIDICE

Lemnos

Scione

MACEDONIA

EPIRUS

Corcyra

Epidamnos

Civil war 427

THESSALY

Naupactus

ACHAEA

ELIS

Mantinea

Pylos

Corinth

ARGOS

Sparta

Defeat 406

Ephesus

Notium

Miletus

Samos

Chios

Naxos

Paros

Melos

Thera

Rhodes

City founded 410

Revolt 416

Pericles dies 429
Oligarchic revolution 411-410
Capitulation 404

Sphacteria captured 425

Mytilene

Lesbos

Arginusae

Victory 411

Defeat 424

Seized by Sparta 413

BOEOTIA

Delium

Plataea

Decelea

Athens

EUBOEA

Naval victory 429

Defeat of land-alliance 418

Athenian force sent to Sicily 427. Disastrous expedition to Sicily 414 - 413

to Sicily

Athens and her allies

Sparta and her allies

Note: references to 'victory', 'defeat' are from the Athenian point of view

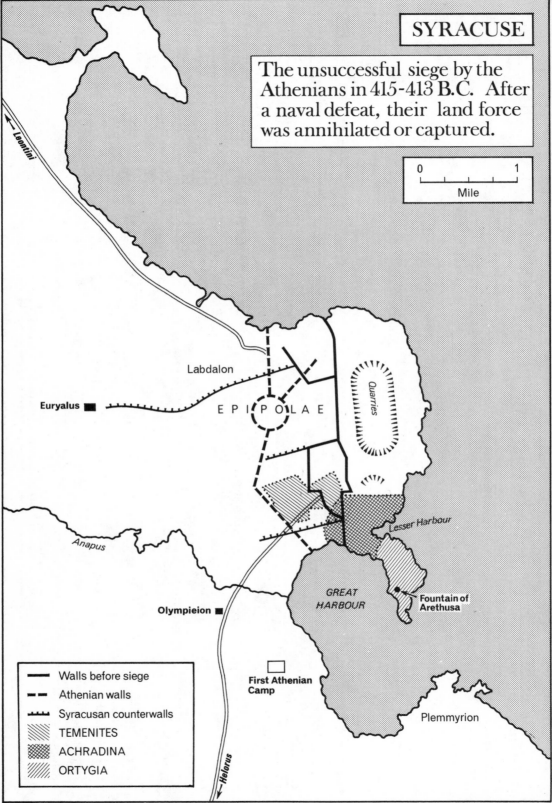

SYRACUSE

The unsuccessful siege by the Athenians in 415-413 B.C. After a naval defeat, their land force was annihilated or captured.

0   1
Mile

Leontini

Labdalon

Euryalus ■

E P I P O L A E

Quarries

Anapus

Lesser Harbour

Olympieion ■

GREAT HARBOUR

Fountain of Arethusa

First Athenian Camp

Plemmyrion

— Walls before siege
– – Athenian walls
┴┴┴ Syracusan counterwalls
▨ TEMENITES
▨ ACHRADINA
▨ ORTYGIA

Helorus

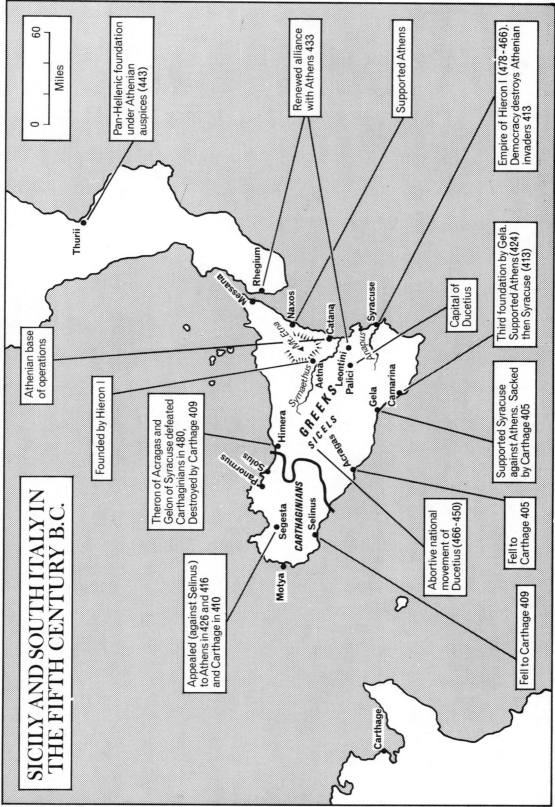

SICILY AND SOUTH ITALY IN THE FIFTH CENTURY B.C.

0 — 60
Miles

Pan-Hellenic foundation under Athenian auspices (443)

Renewed alliance with Athens 433

Supported Athens

Empire of Hieron I (478–466). Democracy destroys Athenian invaders 413

Athenian base of operations

Founded by Hieron I

Theron of Acragas and Gelon of Syracuse defeated Carthaginians in 480, Destroyed by Carthage 409

Capital of Ducetius

Third foundation by Gela. Supported Athens (424) then Syracuse (413)

Supported Syracuse against Athens. Sacked by Carthage 405

Abortive national movement of Ducetius (466–450)

Fell to Carthage 405

Appealed (against Selinus) to Athens in 426 and 416 and Carthage in 410

Fell to Carthage 409

Thurii

Messana

Rhegium

Naxos

Catana

Mt. Etna

Syracuse

Anapus

Symaethus

Aetna

Leontini

Palici

GREEKS

SICELS

Gela

Camarina

Himera

Solus

Panormus

Acragas

Segesta

Selinus

CARTHAGINIANS

Motya

Carthage

31

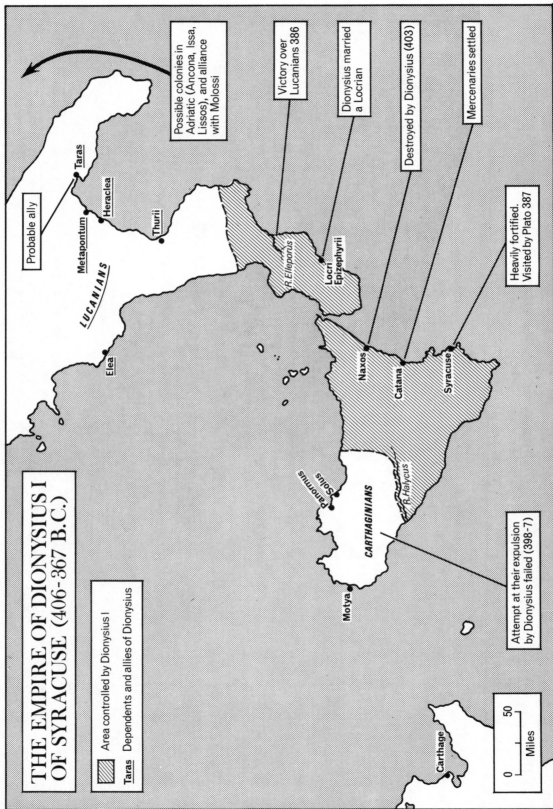

THE EMPIRE OF DIONYSIUS I OF SYRACUSE (406-367 B.C.)

Area controlled by Dionysius I

Taras Dependents and allies of Dionysius

Possible colonies in Adriatic (Ancona, Issa, Lissos), and alliance with Molossi

Victory over Lucanians 386

Dionysius married a Locrian

Destroyed by Dionysius (403)

Mercenaries settled

Heavily fortified. Visited by Plato 387

Probable ally

Taras

Heraclea

Metapontum

Thurii

LUCANIANS

Elea

R. Elleporus

Locri Epizephyrii

Naxos

Catana

Syracuse

Panormus

Solus

R. Halycus

CARTHAGINIANS

Motya

Attempt at their expulsion by Dionysius failed (398-7)

Carthage

50

0

Miles

32

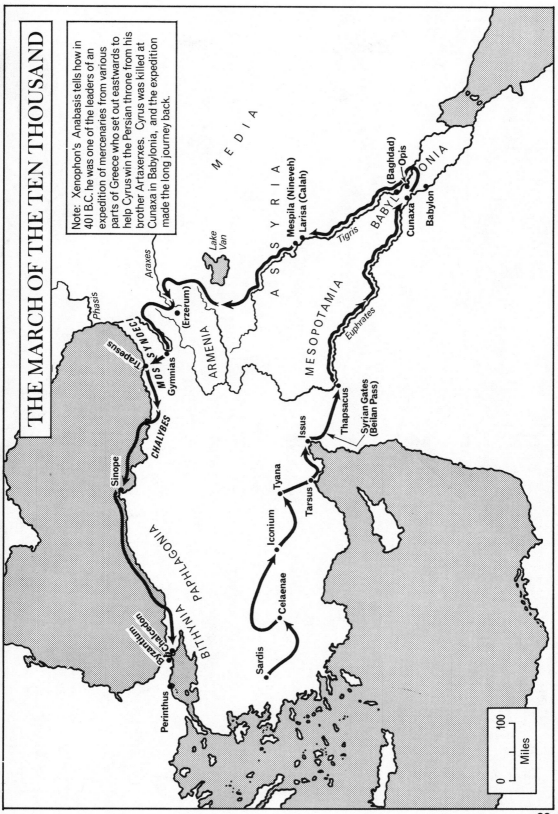

THE MARCH OF THE TEN THOUSAND

Note: Xenophon's Anabasis tells how in 401 B.C. he was one of the leaders of an expedition of mercenaries from various parts of Greece who set out eastwards to help Cyrus win the Persian throne from his brother Artaxerxes. Cyrus was killed at Cunaxa in Babylonia, and the expedition made the long journey back.

MEDIA

Lake Van

ASSYRIA

Mespila (Nineveh)

Larisa (Calah)

Tigris

Araxes

(Erzerum)

ARMENIA

MESOPOTAMIA

Euphrates

BABYLONIA

(Baghdad)

Opis

Cunaxa

Babylon

Phasis

MOSSYNOECI

Trapezus

CHALYBES

Gymnias

Sinope

Thapsacus

Syrian Gates (Beilan Pass)

Issus

BITHYNIA

PAPHLAGONIA

Tyana

Iconium

Tarsus

Byzantium

Chalcedon

Celaenae

Perinthus

Sardis

0	100
Miles	

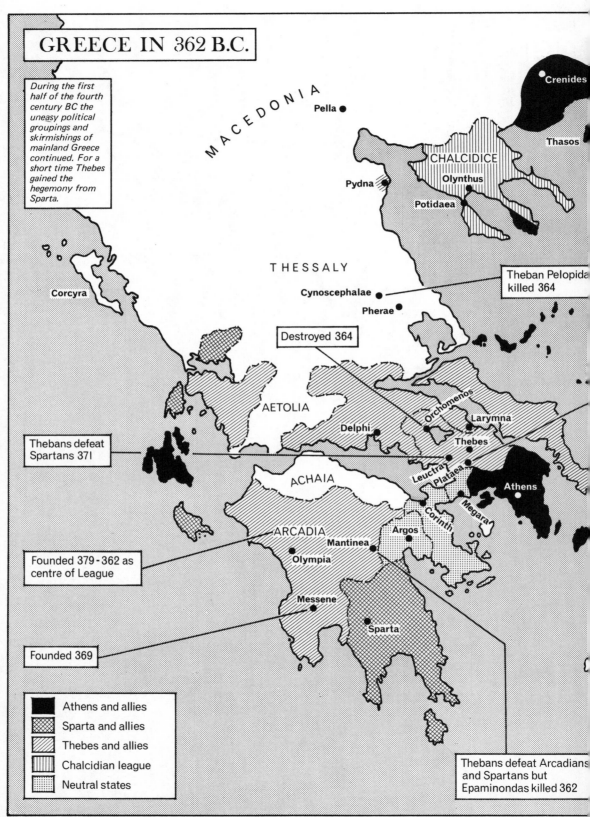

GREECE IN 362 B.C.

During the first half of the fourth century BC the uneasy political groupings and skirmishings of mainland Greece continued. For a short time Thebes gained the hegemony from Sparta.

MACEDONIA

Crenides

Pella

Thasos

CHALCIDICE

Olynthus

Pydna

Potidaea

THESSALY

Theban Pelopidas killed 364

Cynoscephalae

Pherae

Destroyed 364

Corcyra

AETOLIA

Orchomenos

Larymna

Delphi

Thebes

Thebans defeat Spartans 371

Leuctra

Plataea

Athens

ACHAIA

Corinth

Megara

ARCADIA

Argos

Mantinea

Founded 379-362 as centre of League

Olympia

Messene

Sparta

Founded 369

	Athens and allies
	Sparta and allies
	Thebes and allies
	Chalcidian league
	Neutral states

Thebans defeat Arcadians and Spartans but Epaminondas killed 362

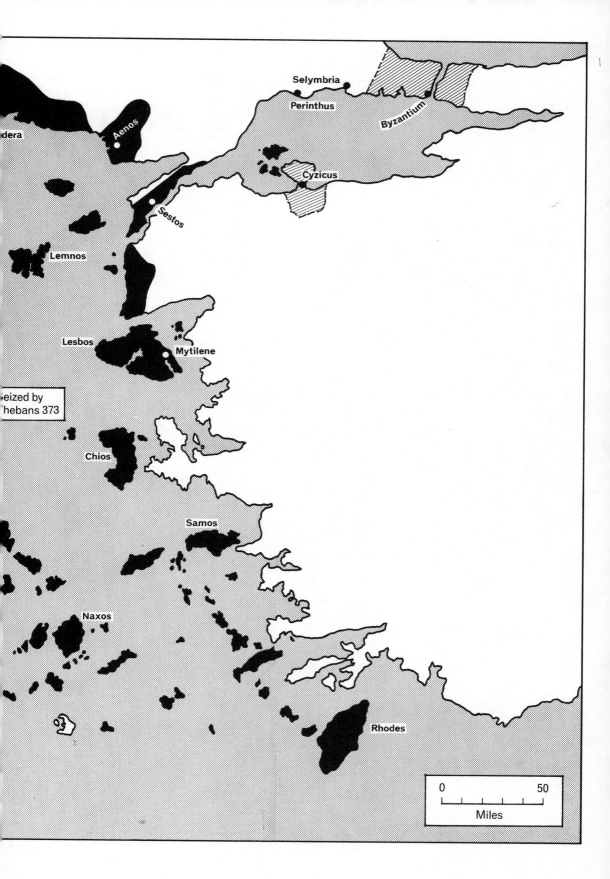

Selymbria

Perinthus

Byzantium

dera

Aenos

Cyzicus

Sestos

Lemnos

Lesbos

Mytilene

Seized by
Thebans 373

Chios

Samos

Naxos

Rhodes

0   50

Miles

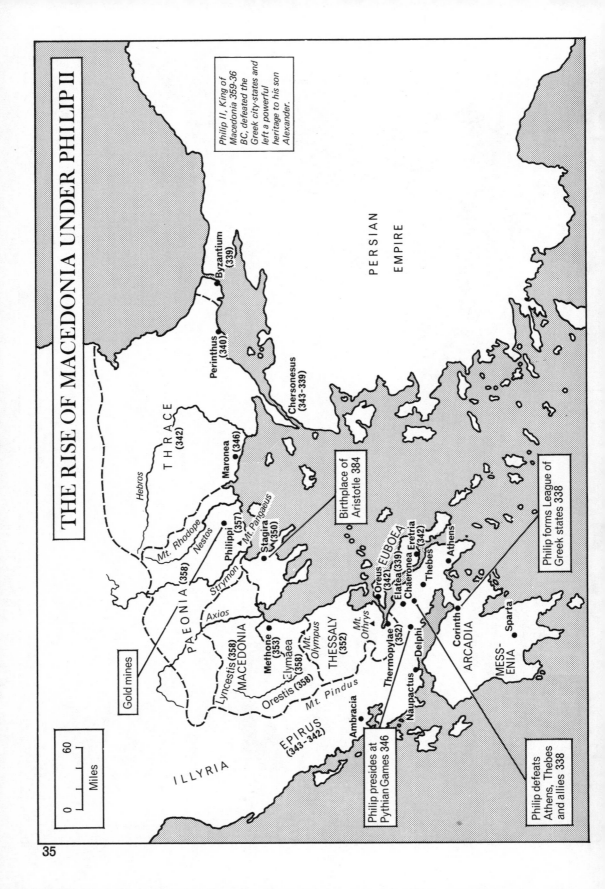

THE RISE OF MACEDONIA UNDER PHILIP II

Philip II, King of Macedonia 359-36 BC, defeated the Greek city-states and left a powerful heritage to his son Alexander.

PERSIAN EMPIRE

Byzantium (339)

Perinthus (340)

Chersonesus (343-339)

THRACE (342)

Hebros

Maronea (346)

Mt. Rhodope

Nestos

Philippi (357)

Mt. Pangaeus

Stagira (350)

Birthplace of Aristotle 384

EUBOEA

Oreus (342)

Elatea (339)

Chaeronea

Eretria (342)

Athens

Thebes

Philip forms League of Greek states 338

Gold mines

Strymon

Axios

PAEONIA (358)

Lyncestis (358)

MACEDONIA

Methone (353)

Elymaea

Orestis (358)

Mt. Olympus

Mt. Othrys

THESSALY (352)

Thermopylae (352)

Delphi

Naupactus

Corinth

ARCADIA

MESS-ENIA

Sparta

Mt. Pindus

EPIRUS (343-342)

Ambracia

ILLYRIA

Philip presides at Pythian Games 346

Philip defeats Athens, Thebes and allies 338

Miles

0   60

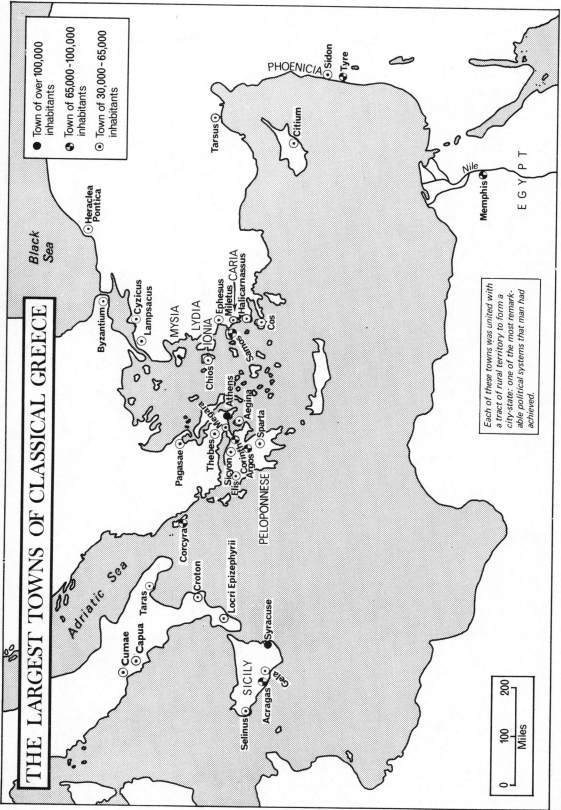

THE LARGEST TOWNS OF CLASSICAL GREECE

Legend:
- ● Town of over 100,000 inhabitants
- ◑ Town of 65,000 - 100,000 inhabitants
- ◉ Town of 30,000 - 65,000 inhabitants

Each of these towns was united with a tract of rural territory to form a city-state: one of the most remarkable political systems that man had achieved.

Black Sea

PHOENICIA
Sidon
Tyre

Tarsus

Citium

Nile

E G Y P T

Memphis

Heraclea Pontica

Cyzicus
Lampsacus

Byzantium

MYSIA

LYDIA
Ephesus
Miletus CARIA
Halicarnassus

IONIA

Cos

Chios

Samos

Athens
Megara
Aegina
Sparta

Thebes
Sicyon
Corinth
Argos

Pagasae

Elis

PELOPONNESE

Corcyra

Croton

Locri Epizephyrii

Taras
Capua
Cumae

Syracuse

SICILY
Gela
Acragas
Selinus

Adriatic Sea

0   100   200
Miles

36

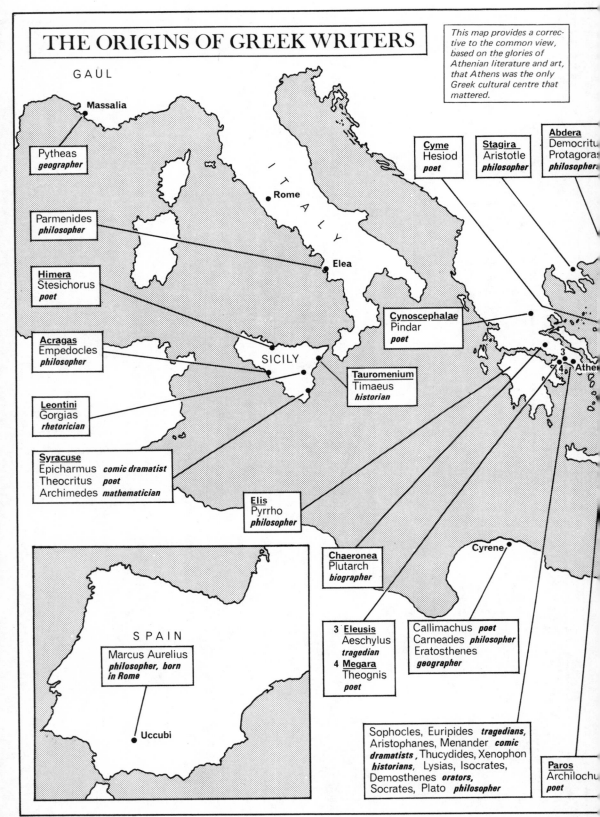

THE ORIGINS OF GREEK WRITERS

This map provides a corrective to the common view, based on the glories of Athenian literature and art, that Athens was the only Greek cultural centre that mattered.

GAUL

Massalia

Pytheas
geographer

ITALY

Rome

Parmenides
philosopher

Elea

Himera
Stesichorus
poet

Cyme
Hesiod
poet

Stagira
Aristotle
philosopher

Abdera
Democritus
Protagoras
philosophers

Cynoscephalae
Pindar
poet

Acragas
Empedocles
philosopher

SICILY

Tauromenium
Timaeus
historian

3
4
Athens

Leontini
Gorgias
rhetorician

Syracuse
Epicharmus   *comic dramatist*
Theocritus   *poet*
Archimedes   *mathematician*

Elis
Pyrrho
philosopher

Chaeronea
Plutarch
biographer

Cyrene

SPAIN

Marcus Aurelius
*philosopher, born
in Rome*

Uccubi

3 **Eleusis**
Aeschylus
tragedian
4 **Megara**
Theognis
poet

Callimachus *poet*
Carneades *philosopher*
Eratosthenes
geographer

Paros
Archilochus
poet

Sophocles, Euripides *tragedians,*
Aristophanes, Menander *comic
dramatists ,* Thucydides, Xenophon
historians, Lysias, Isocrates,
Demosthenes *orators,*
Socrates, Plato *philosopher*

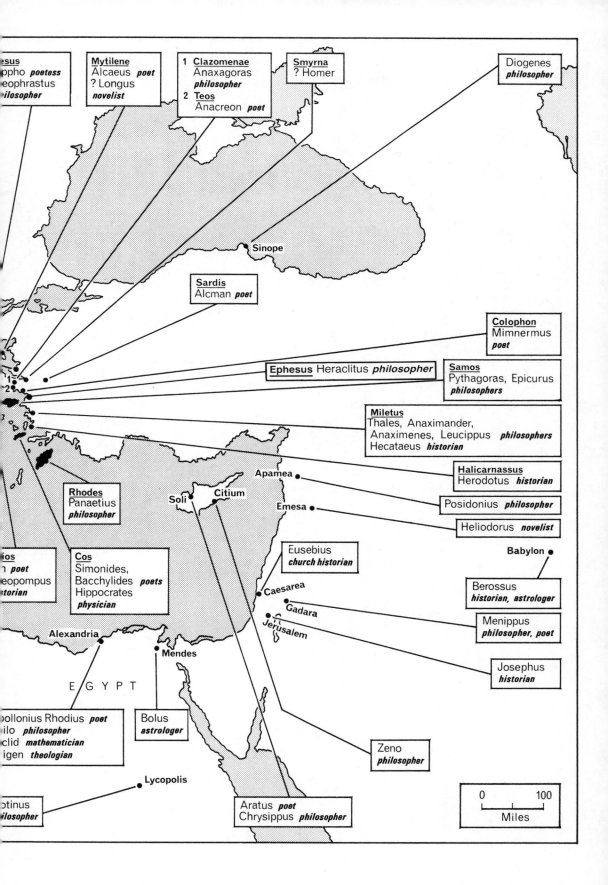

[esus
ppho *poetess*
eophrastus
ilosopher

Mytilene
Alcaeus *poet*
? Longus
novelist

1 **Clazomenae**
Anaxagoras
philosopher
2 **Teos**
Anacreon *poet*

Smyrna
? Homer

Diogenes
philosopher

Sinope

Sardis
Alcman *poet*

Colophon
Mimnermus
poet

Ephesus Heraclitus *philosopher*

Samos
Pythagoras, Epicurus
philosophers

Miletus
Thales, Anaximander,
Anaximenes, Leucippus *philosophers*
Hecataeus *historian*

Apamea

Halicarnassus
Herodotus *historian*

Soli   Citium

Emesa

Posidonius *philosopher*

Heliodorus *novelist*

Rhodes
Panaetius
philosopher

Babylon

ios
poet
eopompus
torian

Cos
Simonides,
Bacchylides *poets*
Hippocrates
physician

Eusebius
church historian

Berossus
historian, astrologer

Caesarea

Gadara

Menippus
philosopher, poet

Alexandria

Jerusalem

Josephus
historian

Mendes

E G Y P T

pollonius Rhodius *poet*
ilo *philosopher*
clid *mathematician*
igen *theologian*

Bolus
astrologer

Zeno
philosopher

Lycopolis

otinus
ilosopher

Aratus *poet*
Chrysippus *philosopher*

0   100
Miles

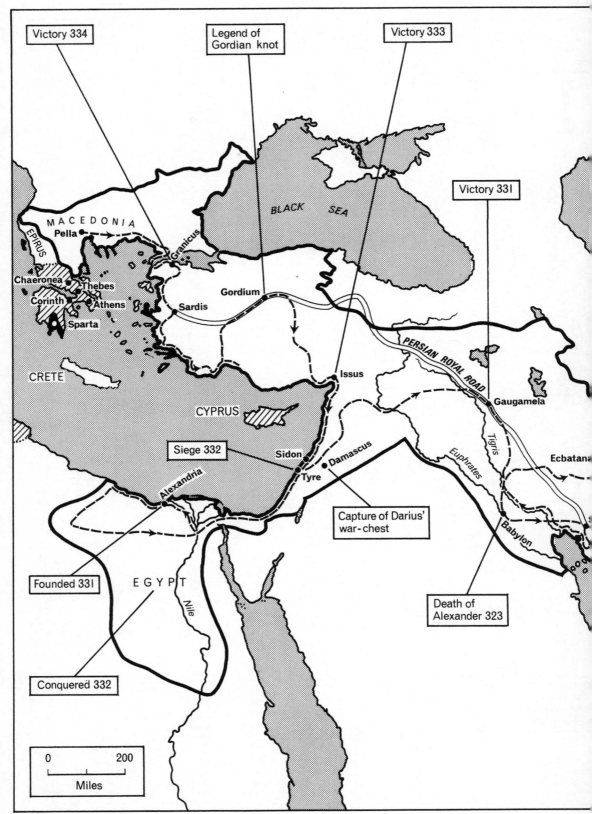

Victory 334

Legend of
Gordian knot

Victory 333

Victory 331

MACEDONIA

Pella

EPIRUS

Granicus

BLACK SEA

Chaeronea

Thebes

Corinth

Athens

Gordium

Sparta

Sardis

PERSIAN ROYAL ROAD

Gaugamela

CRETE

Issus

CYPRUS

Tigris

Ecbatana

Siege 332

Sidon

Damascus

Euphrates

Tyre

Alexandria

Babylon

Capture of Darius'
war-chest

Founded 331

EGYPT

Nile

Death of
Alexander 323

Conquered 332

0   200

Miles

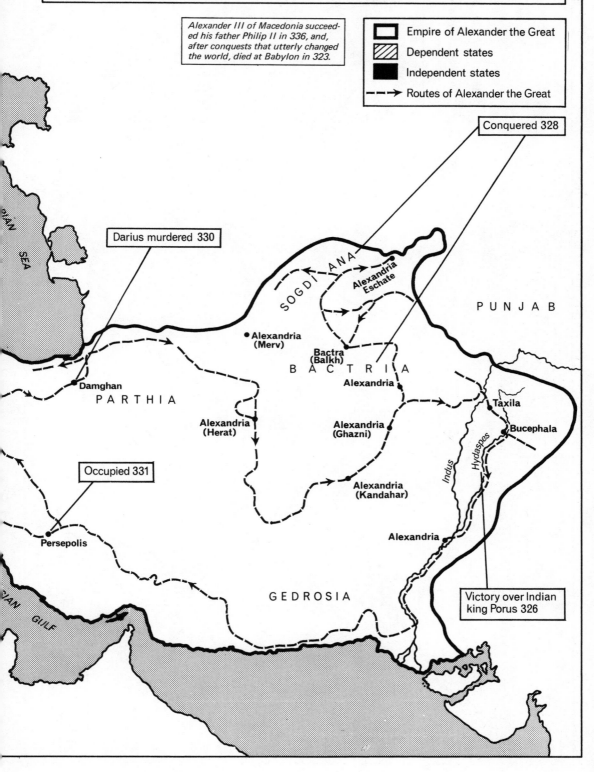

THE CONQUESTS OF ALEXANDER THE GREAT

Alexander III of Macedonia succeeded his father Philip II in 336, and, after conquests that utterly changed the world, died at Babylon in 323.

☐ Empire of Alexander the Great
▨ Dependent states
■ Independent states
– – –▶ Routes of Alexander the Great

Conquered 328

Darius murdered 330

CASPIAN SEA

SOGDIANA

Alexandria Eschate

PUNJAB

Alexandria (Merv)

Bactra (Balkh)

BACTRIA

Alexandria

Damghan

PARTHIA

Taxila

Bucephala

Alexandria (Herat)

Alexandria (Ghazni)

Indus

Hydaspes

Occupied 331

Alexandria (Kandahar)

Persepolis

Alexandria

PERSIAN GULF

GEDROSIA

Victory over Indian king Porus 326

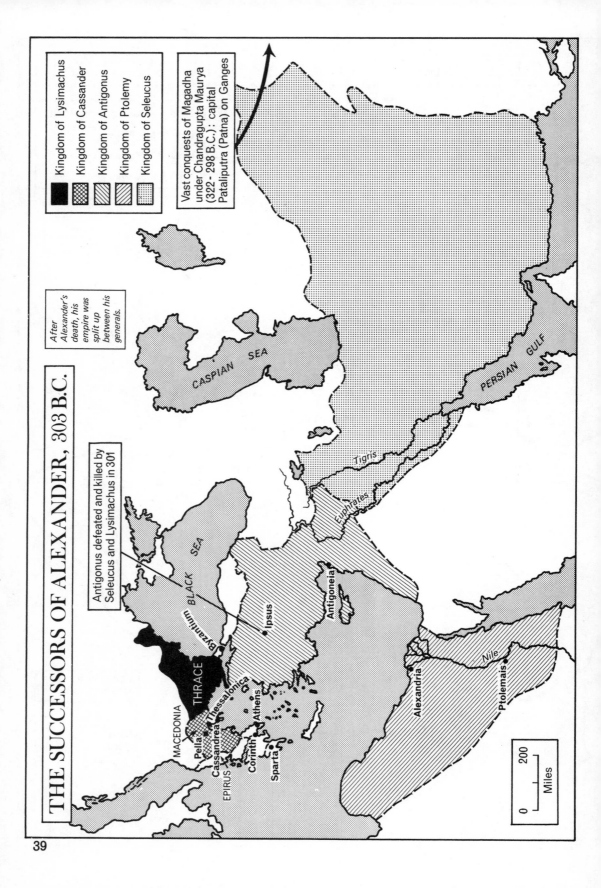

THE SUCCESSORS OF ALEXANDER, 303 B.C.

Kingdom of Lysimachus
Kingdom of Cassander
Kingdom of Antigonus
Kingdom of Ptolemy
Kingdom of Seleucus

Vast conquests of Magadha under Chandragupta Maurya (322 - 298 B.C.): capital Pataliputra (Patna) on Ganges

After Alexander's death, his empire was split up between his generals.

Antigonus defeated and killed by Seleucus and Lysimachus in 301

CASPIAN SEA

PERSIAN GULF

Tigris

Euphrates

BLACK SEA

Byzantium

Ipsus

Antigoneia

Nile

THRACE

MACEDONIA

Pella

Thessalonica

Cassandrea

EPIRUS

Corinth

Athens

Sparta

Alexandria

Ptolemais

0   200
Miles

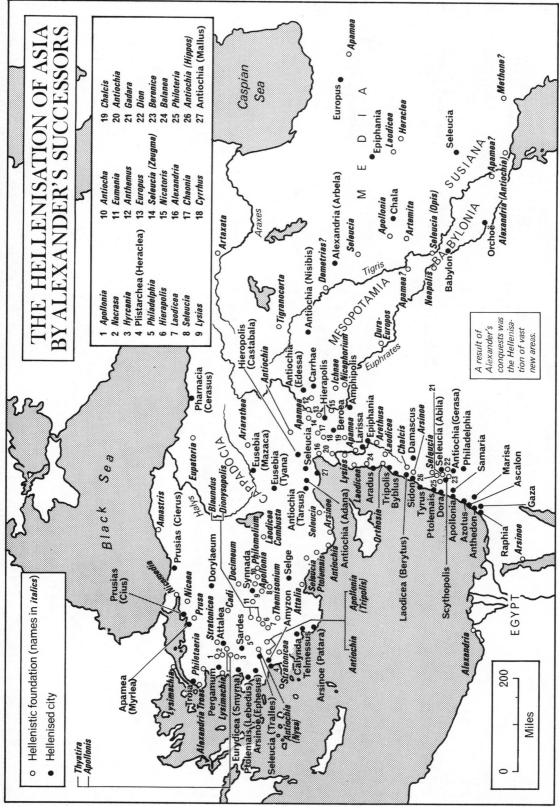

THE HELLENISATION OF ASIA BY ALEXANDER'S SUCCESSORS

1 *Apollonia*
2 *Nacrasa*
3 *Hyrcania*
4 *Plistarchea (Heraclea)*
5 *Philadelphia*
6 *Hierapolis*
7 *Laodicea*
8 *Seleucia*
9 *Lysias*

10 *Antiocha*
11 *Eumenia*
12 *Anthemus*
13 *Europus*
14 *Seleucia (Zeugma)*
15 *Nicatoris*
16 *Alexandria*
17 *Chaonia*
18 *Cyrrhus*

19 *Chalcis*
20 *Antiochia*
21 *Gadara*
22 *Dion*
23 *Berenice*
24 *Balanea*
25 *Philoteria*
26 *Antiochia (Hippos)*
27 *Antiochia (Mallus)*

○ Hellenistic foundation (names in *italics*)
● Hellenised city

Thyatira
― Apollonis

A result of Alexander's conquests was the Hellenisation of vast new areas.

200
Miles
0

Caspian Sea

Black Sea

EGYPT

MEDIA

MESOPOTAMIA

SUSIANA

BABYLONIA

CAPPADOCIA

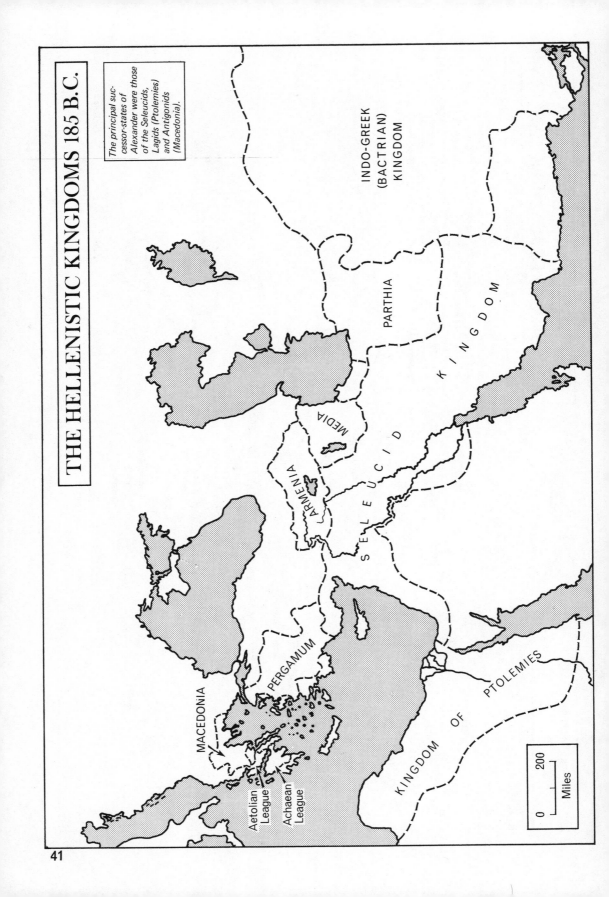

THE HELLENISTIC KINGDOMS 185 B.C.

The principal successor-states of Alexander were those of the Seleucids, Lagids (Ptolemies) and Antigonids (Macedonia).

INDO-GREEK (BACTRIAN) KINGDOM

PARTHIA

SELEUCID KINGDOM

MEDIA

ARMENIA

PERGAMUM

MACEDONIA

Aetolian League

Achaean League

KINGDOM OF PTOLEMIES

0   200

Miles

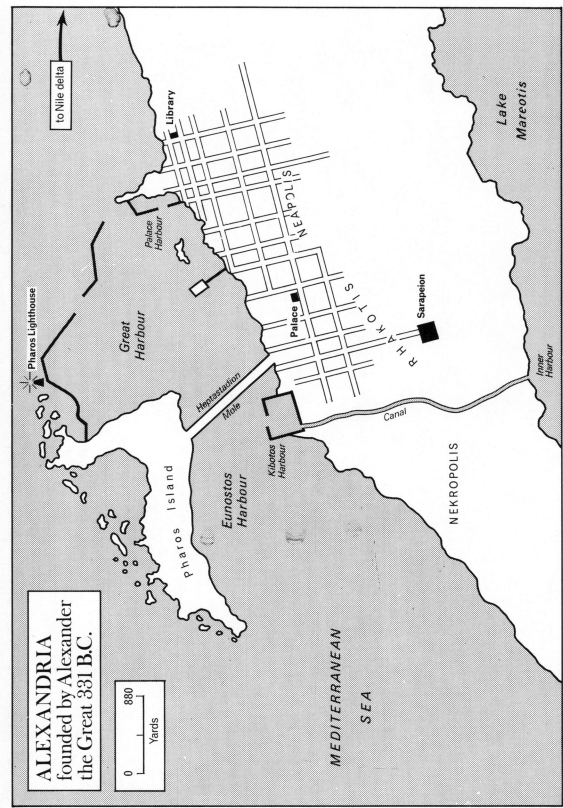

ALEXANDRIA
founded by Alexander
the Great 331 B.C.

0   880
      Yards

to Nile delta

Pharos Lighthouse

Library

Palace Harbour

Great Harbour

Heptastadion

Mole

Pharos Island

Eunostos Harbour

Kibotos Harbour

MEDITERRANEAN SEA

NEAPOLIS

R H A K O T I S

Palace

Sarapeion

Canal

Inner Harbour

Lake Mareotis

NEKROPOLIS

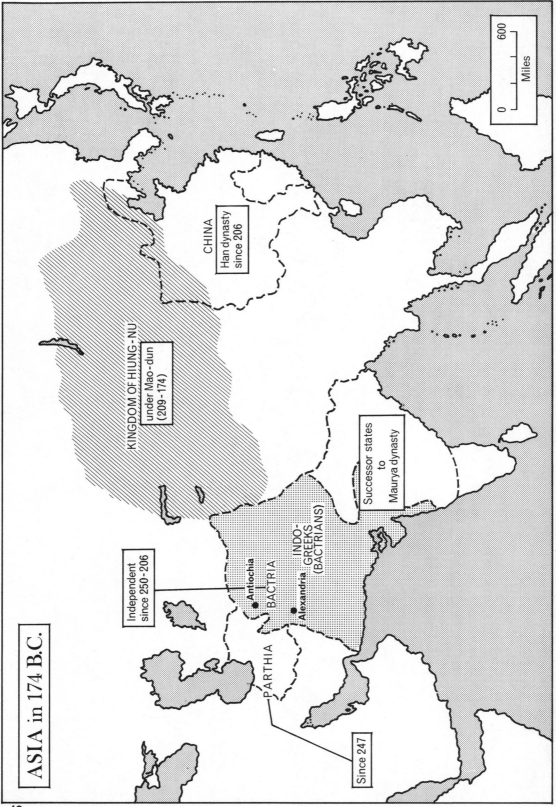

ASIA in 174 B.C.

KINGDOM OF HIUNG-NU
under Mao-dun
(209-174)

CHINA
Han dynasty
since 206

Successor states
to
Maurya dynasty

Independent
since 250-206

INDO-
GREEKS
(BACTRIANS)

Antiochia
BACTRIA

Alexandria

PARTHIA

Since 247

600
Miles
0

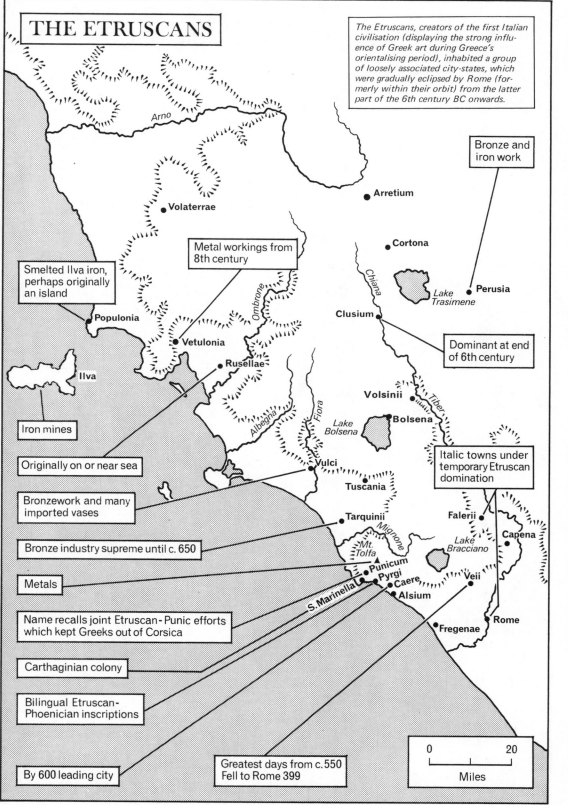

THE ETRUSCANS

The Etruscans, creators of the first Italian civilisation (displaying the strong influence of Greek art during Greece's orientalising period), inhabited a group of loosely associated city-states, which were gradually eclipsed by Rome (formerly within their orbit) from the latter part of the 6th century BC onwards.

Arno

Bronze and iron work

• **Volaterrae**

• **Arretium**

Metal workings from 8th century

• **Cortona**

Chiana

Smelted Ilva iron, perhaps originally an island

Ombrone

• **Perusia**

Lake Trasimene

Populonia

• **Vetulonia**

Clusium

Dominant at end of 6th century

Ilva

• **Rusellae**

Iron mines

Albegna

Fiora

Volsinii

• **Bolsena**

Tiber

Lake Bolsena

Originally on or near sea

Italic towns under temporary Etruscan domination

Vulci

Bronzework and many imported vases

Tuscania

Falerii

Lake Bracciano

Capena

Bronze industry supreme until c. 650

Mignone

Tarquinii

Mt. Tolfa

Metals

Punicum
Pyrgi
Caere
Veii

Name recalls joint Etruscan-Punic efforts which kept Greeks out of Corsica

S. Marinella

Alsium

Rome

Carthaginian colony

• **Fregenae**

Bilingual Etruscan-Phoenician inscriptions

By 600 leading city

Greatest days from c. 550
Fell to Rome 399

0   20

Miles

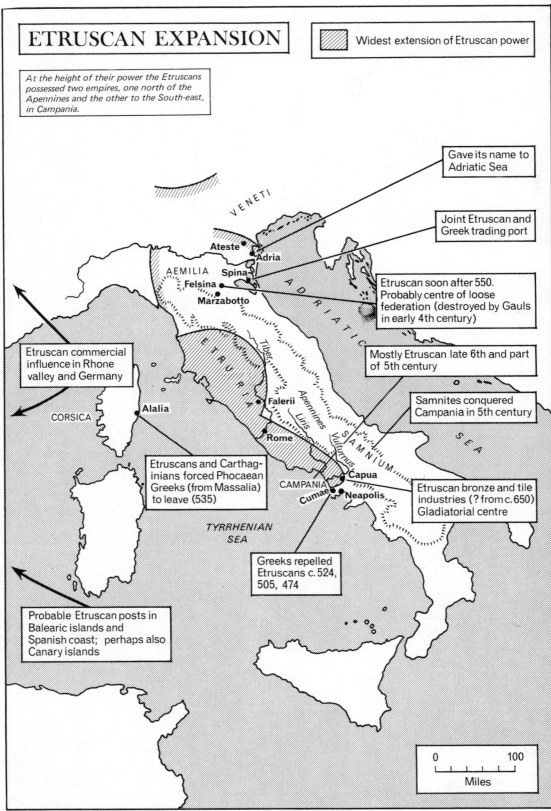

ETRUSCAN EXPANSION

Widest extension of Etruscan power

At the height of their power the Etruscans possessed two empires, one north of the Apennines and the other to the South-east, in Campania.

Gave its name to Adriatic Sea

Joint Etruscan and Greek trading port

Etruscan soon after 550. Probably centre of loose federation (destroyed by Gauls in early 4th century)

Mostly Etruscan late 6th and part of 5th century

Samnites conquered Campania in 5th century

Etruscan commercial influence in Rhone valley and Germany

Etruscans and Carthaginians forced Phocaean Greeks (from Massalia) to leave (535)

Etruscan bronze and tile industries (? from c. 650) Gladiatorial centre

Greeks repelled Etruscans c. 524, 505, 474

Probable Etruscan posts in Balearic islands and Spanish coast; perhaps also Canary islands

VENETI

Ateste
Adria
AEMILIA
Spina
Felsina
Marzabotto
ETRURIA
Tiber
Apennines
ADRIATIC
Falerii
Liris
Rome
SAMNIUM
Vulturnus
Capua
CAMPANIA
Cumae
Neapolis
SEA

CORSICA
Alalia

TYRRHENIAN
SEA

0   100

Miles

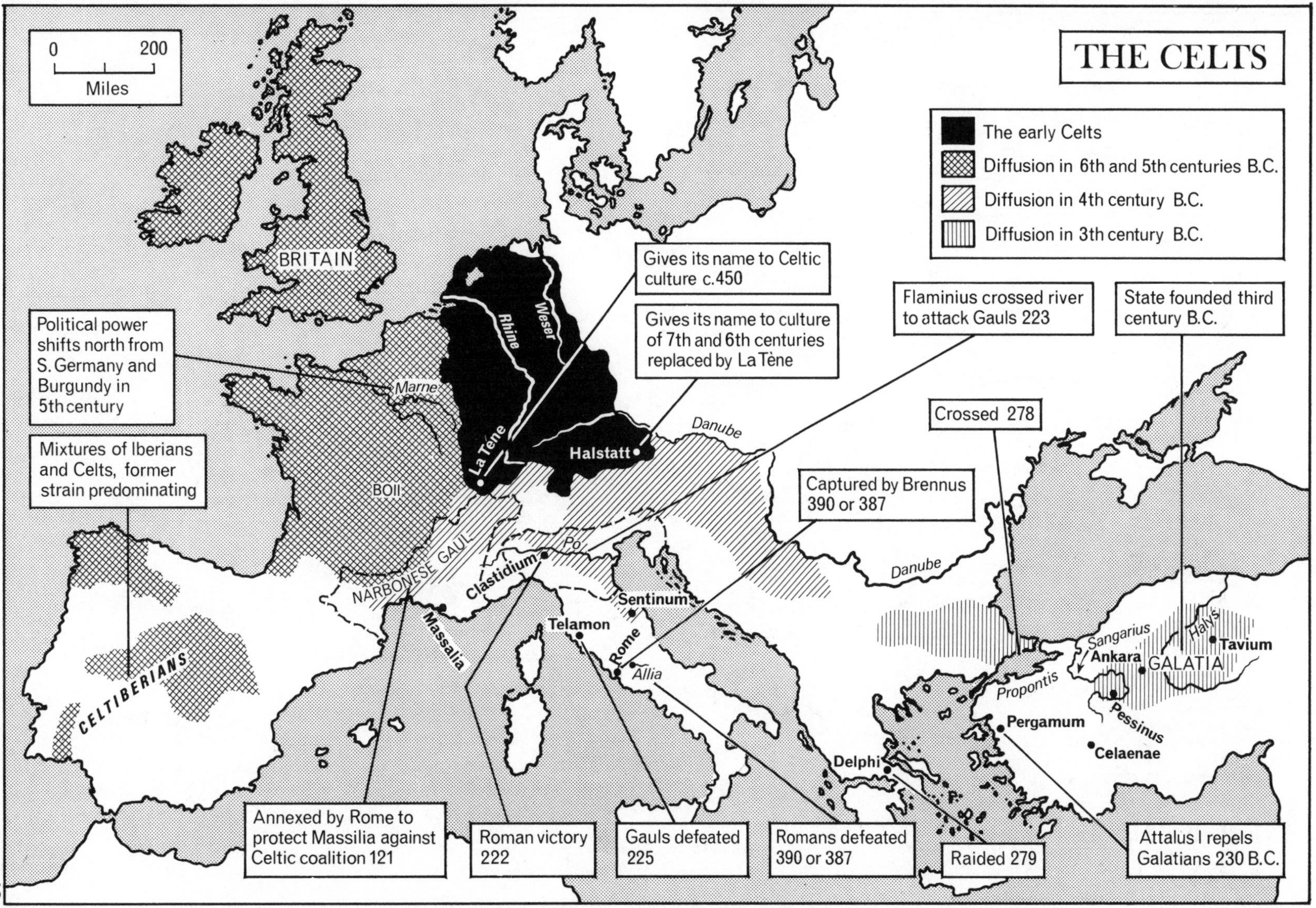

THE CELTS
0 200
Miles
The early Celts
Diffusion in 6th and 5th centuries B.C.
Diffusion in 4th century B.C.
Diffusion in 3th century B.C.
BRITAIN
Rhine
Weser
Marne
La Tène
Halstatt
Danube
BOII
NARBONESE GAUL
Po
Clastidium
Massalia
Sentinum
Telamon
Rome
Allia
CELTIBERIANS
Delphi
Propontis
Sangarius
Halys
Ankara
GALATIA
Tavium
Pessinus
Pergamum
Celaenae
Gives its name to Celtic culture c.450
Gives its name to culture of 7th and 6th centuries replaced by La Tène
Political power shifts north from S. Germany and Burgundy in 5th century
Mixtures of Iberians and Celts, former strain predominating
Flaminius crossed river to attack Gauls 223
State founded third century B.C.
Crossed 278
Captured by Brennus 390 or 387
Annexed by Rome to protect Massilia against Celtic coalition 121
Roman victory 222
Gauls defeated 225
Romans defeated 390 or 387
Raided 279
Attalus I repels Galatians 230 B.C.

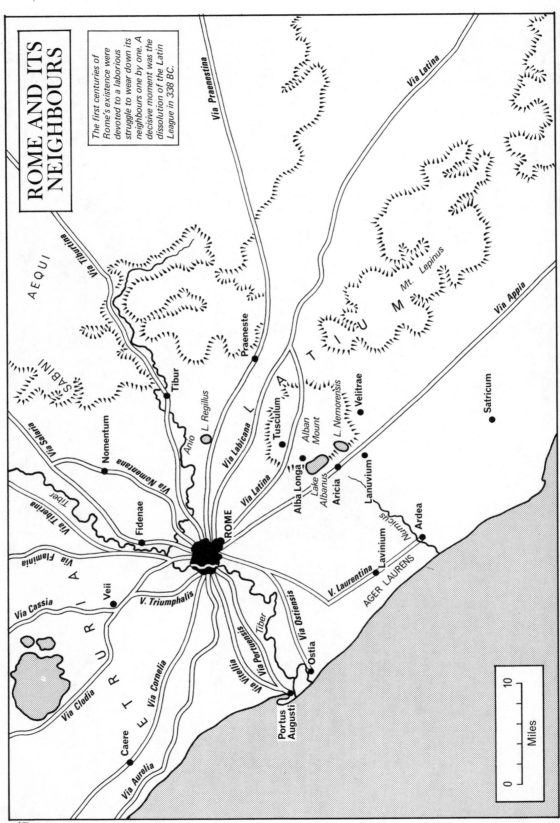

ROME AND ITS NEIGHBOURS

The first centuries of Rome's existence were devoted to a laborious struggle to wear down its neighbours one by one. A decisive moment was the dissolution of the Latin League in 338 BC.

Via Praenestina

Via Latina

Via Tiburtina

AEQUI

SABINI

Via Salaria

Via Nomentana

Tibur

L. Regillus

Anio

Nomentum

Via Tiberina

Via Flaminia

Fidenae

Via Cassia

Veii

V. Triumphalis

ROME

Via Labicana

Via Latina

Tusculum

Alban Mount

Alba Longa

Lake Albanus

Aricia

L. Nemorensis

Velitrae

Mt. Lepinus

L A T I U M

Satricum

Via Appia

Lanuvium

Numicus

Ardea

Lavinium

V. Laurentina

AGER LAURENS

E T R U R I A

Via Clodia

Via Cornelia

Caere

Via Aurelia

Via Vitellia

Via Portuensis

Tiber

Via Ostiensis

Ostia

Portus Augusti

Praeneste

10

Miles

0

47

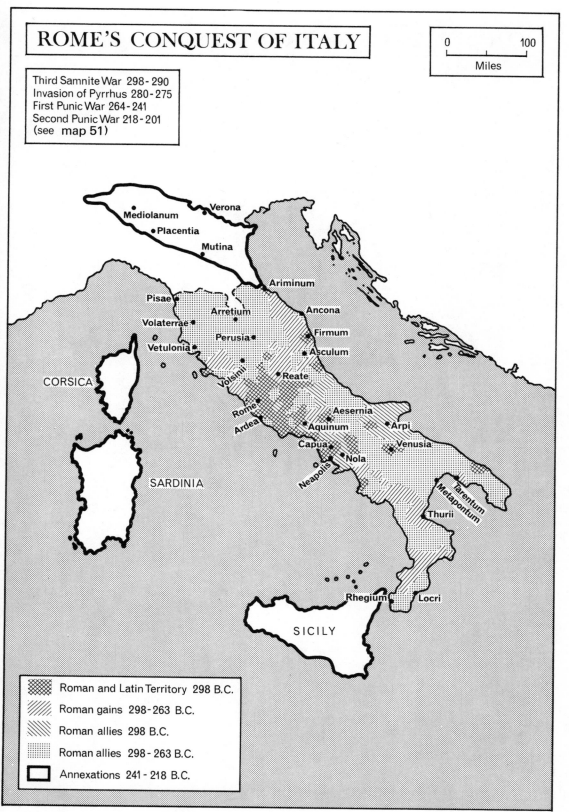

ROME'S CONQUEST OF ITALY

Third Samnite War 298-290
Invasion of Pyrrhus 280-275
First Punic War 264-241
Second Punic War 218-201
(see **map 51**)

0 100
Miles

Mediolanum
Verona
Placentia
Mutina
Ariminum
Pisae
Arretium
Ancona
Volaterrae
Perusia
Firmum
Vetulonia
Asculum
Volsinii
Reate
CORSICA
Rome
Aesernia
Ardea
Aquinum
Arpi
Capua
Venusia
Neapolis
Nola
SARDINIA
Tarentum
Metapontum
Thurii
Rhegium
Locri
SICILY

Roman and Latin Territory 298 B.C.
Roman gains 298-263 B.C.
Roman allies 298 B.C.
Roman allies 298-263 B.C.
Annexations 241-218 B.C.

THE ROADS OF ROMAN ITALY

0   100

Miles

Augusta
Praetoria

Mediolanum

Segusio

Verona

Aquileia

⑥

①

Placentia
Cremona

Dertona ⑥

Mantua

Genua

Ravenna

Po

①

Ariminum

Luna

Florentia

Fanum
Fortunae

⑧

Pisae

Vada
Volaterrana

Arretium

⑪

④

ADRIATIC

⑬

Truentum

Reate

Aternum

CORSICA

③

Tiber

Tibur ⑦ Corfinium

ROME Anagnia

SEA

⑤ Fregellae

② Capua Beneventum

Tarracina

Cales Casilinum ⑩ Canusium

SARDINIA

Neapolis

Venusia ② Brundisium

⑫

Tarentum

⑨

TYRRHENIAN
SEA

Rhegium

S I C I L Y

❶ Via Aemilia (187 B.C.)	❽ Via Julia Augusta
❷ Via Appia (312 - 244 B.C.)	❾ Via Domitiana
❸ Via Aurelia	❿ Via Trajana
❹ Via Flaminia (220 B.C.)	⓫ Via Cassia
❺ Via Latina	⓬ Via Popillia
❻ Via Postumia (148 B.C.)	⓭ Via Salaria
❼ Via Valeria	

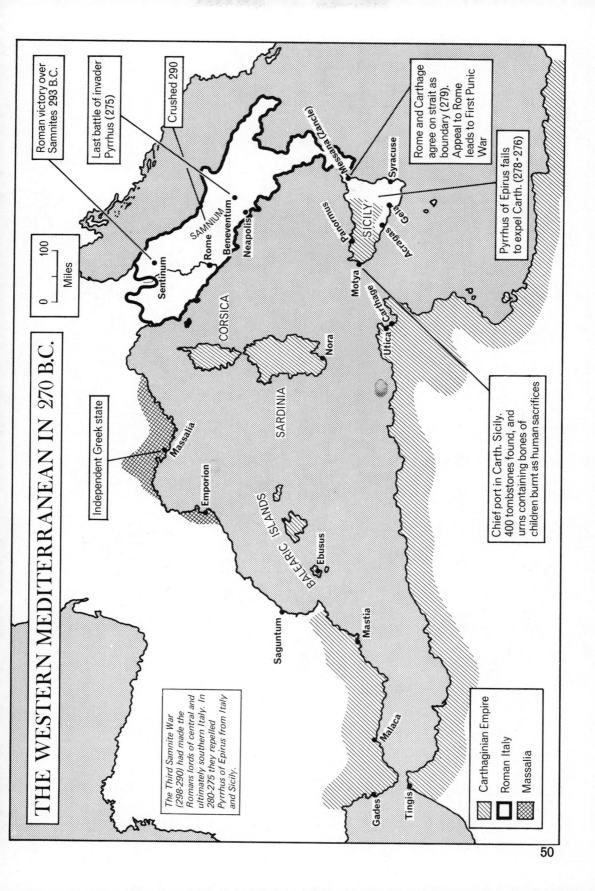

THE WESTERN MEDITERRANEAN IN 270 B.C.

Roman victory over Samnites 293 B.C.

Last battle of invader Pyrrhus (275)

Crushed 290

Rome and Carthage agree on strait as boundary (279). Appeal to Rome leads to First Punic War

Pyrrhus of Epirus fails to expel Carth. (278-276)

Independent Greek state

Chief port in Carth. Sicily. 400 tombstones found, and urns containing bones of children burnt as human sacrifices

The Third Samnite War (298-290) had made the Romans lords of central and ultimately southern Italy. In 280-275 they repelled Pyrrhus of Epirus from Italy and Sicily.

0   100
Miles

SAMNIUM

Rome
Beneventum
Neapolis
Sentinum
Messana (Zancle)
Syracuse
SICILY
Gela
Acragas
Panormus
Motya
Carthage
Utica

CORSICA

SARDINIA
Nora

Massalia

Emporion

BALEARIC ISLANDS

Ebusus

Saguntum

Mastia

Malaca
Gades
Tingis

Carthaginian Empire

Roman Italy

Massalia

50

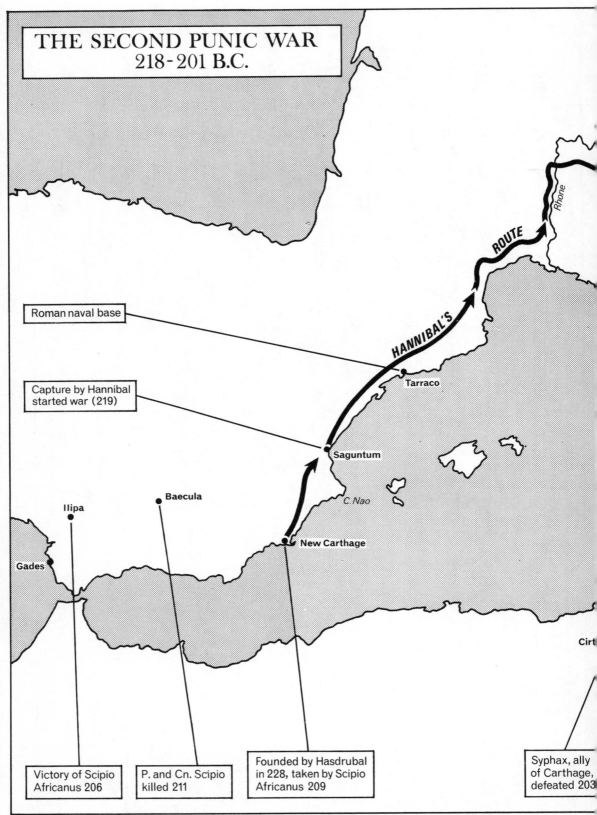

THE SECOND PUNIC WAR
218-201 B.C.

Rhone

HANNIBAL'S ROUTE

Roman naval base

Tarraco

Capture by Hannibal started war (219)

Saguntum

Baecula

Ilipa

C. Nao

New Carthage

Gades

Cirt

Victory of Scipio Africanus 206

P. and Cn. Scipio killed 211

Founded by Hasdrubal in 228, taken by Scipio Africanus 209

Syphax, ally of Carthage, defeated 203

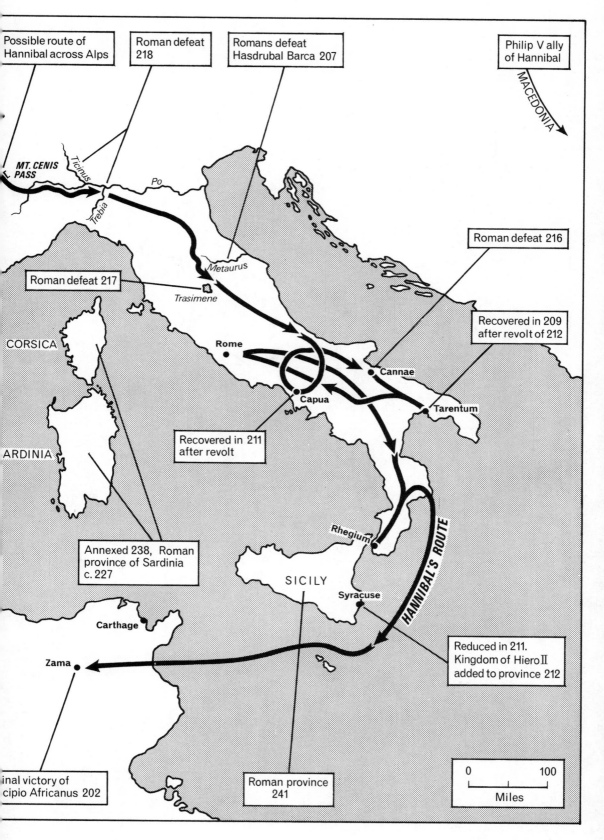

Possible route of
Hannibal across Alps

Roman defeat
218

Romans defeat
Hasdrubal Barca 207

Philip V ally
of Hannibal

MACEDONIA

MT. CENIS
PASS

Ticinus

Po

Trebia

Roman defeat 216

Metaurus

Roman defeat 217

Trasimene

Recovered in 209
after revolt of 212

CORSICA

Rome

Cannae

Capua

Tarentum

Recovered in 211
after revolt

ARDINIA

Annexed 238, Roman
province of Sardinia
c. 227

Rhegium

HANNIBAL'S ROUTE

SICILY

Syracuse

Carthage

Reduced in 211.
Kingdom of Hiero II
added to province 212

Zama

inal victory of
cipio Africanus 202

Roman province
241

0   100

Miles

E

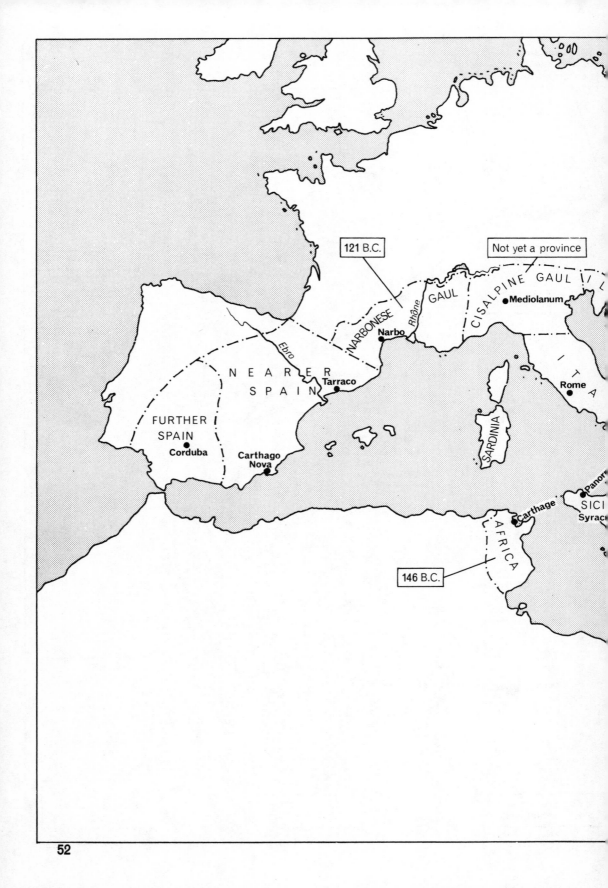

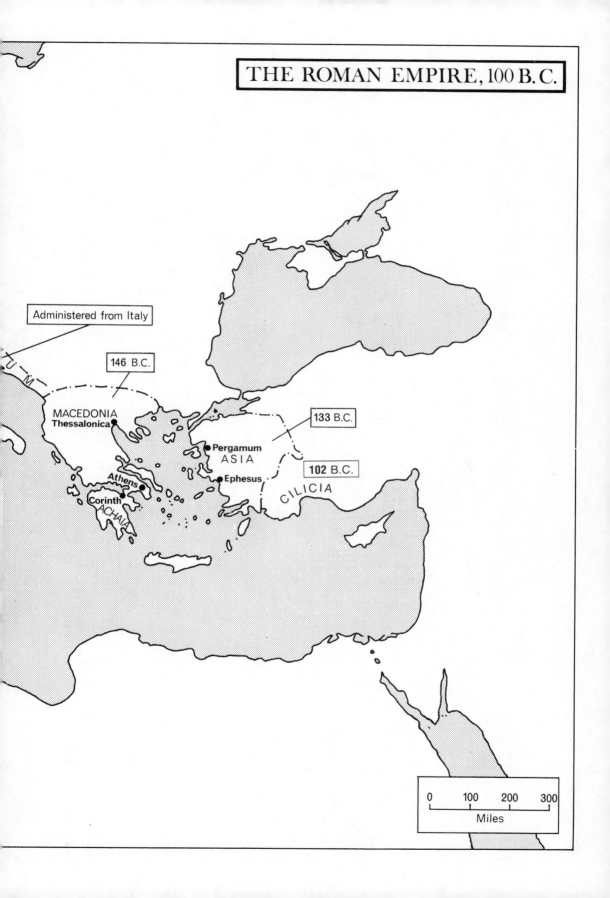

THE ROMAN EMPIRE, 100 B.C.

Administered from Italy

146 B.C.

133 B.C.

MACEDONIA
Thessalonica

102 B.C.

Pergamum
ASIA

Athens

Ephesus

Corinth

CILICIA

ACHAIA

0   100   200   300

Miles

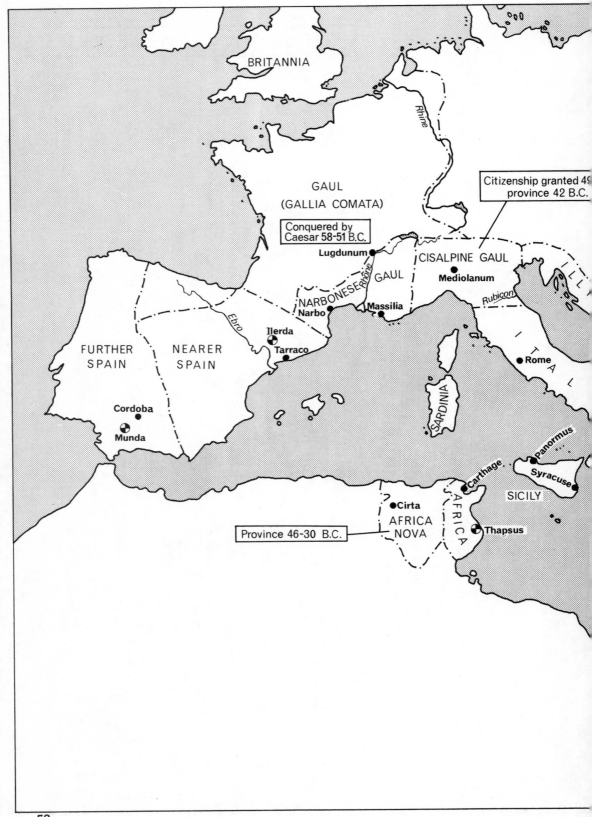

BRITANNIA

GAUL
(GALLIA COMATA)

Conquered by
Caesar 58-51 B.C.

Citizenship granted 49 ...
province 42 B.C.

Lugdunum

GAUL

CISALPINE GAUL

Mediolanum

NARBONESE GAUL

Rubicon

Narbo

Massilia

Ilerda

Tarraco

FURTHER
SPAIN

NEARER
SPAIN

Ebro

Rhône

Rhine

I
T
A
L

Rome

SARDINIA

Cordoba

Munda

Carthage

Panormus

Syracuse

SICILY

Cirta

AFRICA
NOVA

AFRICA

Thapsus

Province 46-30 B.C.

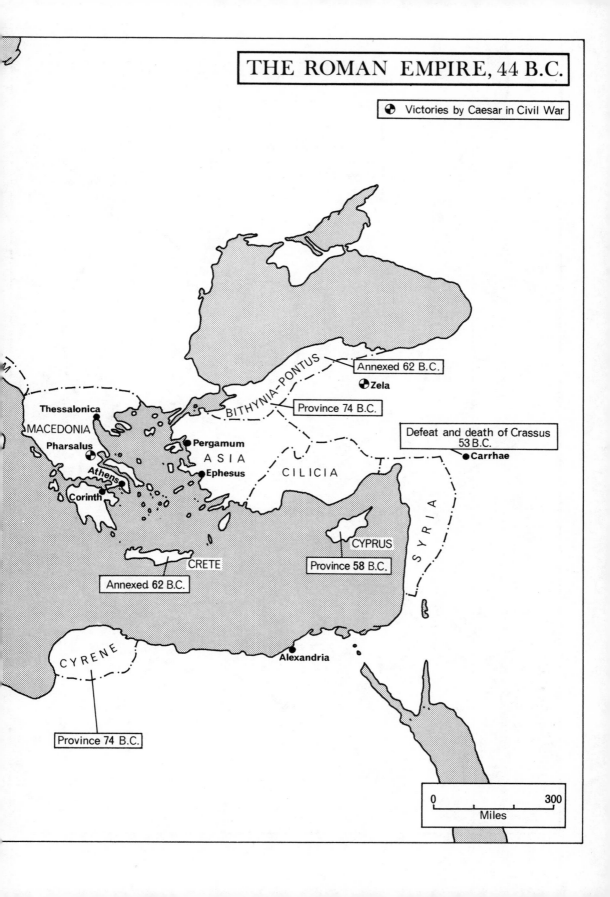

THE ROMAN EMPIRE, 44 B.C.

⊕ Victories by Caesar in Civil War

Annexed 62 B.C.

⊕ Zela

BITHYNIA-PONTUS

Province 74 B.C.

Defeat and death of Crassus
53 B.C.

● Carrhae

Thessalonica

MACEDONIA

Pharsalus

Pergamum

ASIA

Ephesus

CILICIA

Athens

SYRIA

Corinth

CYPRUS

CRETE

Province 58 B.C.

Annexed 62 B.C.

CYRENE

Alexandria

Province 74 B.C.

0   300
Miles

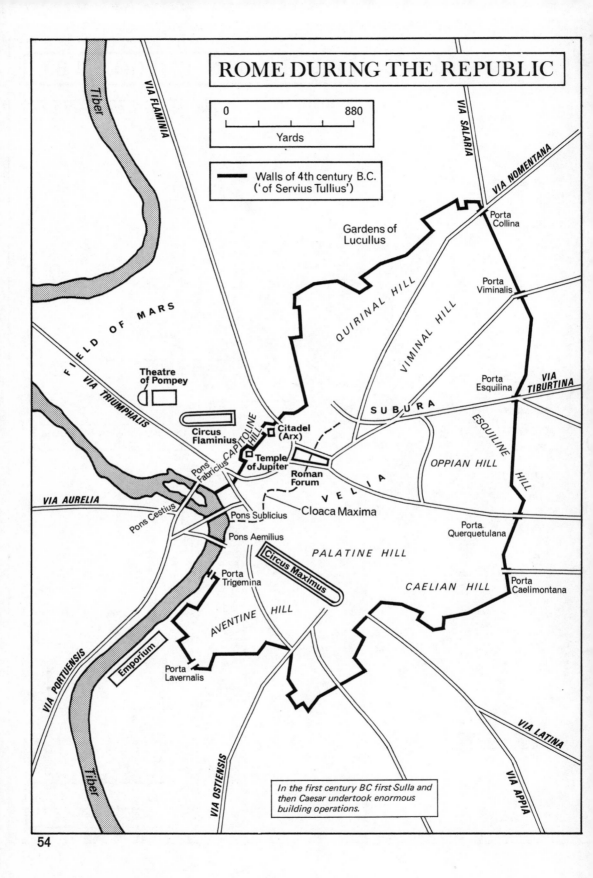

ROME DURING THE REPUBLIC

0 — 880

Yards

Walls of 4th century B.C.
('of Servius Tullius')

Tiber

VIA FLAMINIA

VIA SALARIA

VIA NOMENTANA

Porta
Collina

Gardens of
Lucullus

QUIRINAL HILL

VIMINAL HILL

Porta
Viminalis

F I E L D   O F   M A R S

Porta
Esquilina

VIA
TIBURTINA

VIA TRIUMPHALIS

Theatre
of Pompey

S U B U R A

ESQUILINE
HILL

Circus
Flaminius

CAPITOLINE HILL

Citadel
(Arx)

OPPIAN HILL

Pons
Fabricius

Temple
of Jupiter

Roman
Forum

V E L I A

VIA AURELIA

Pons Cestius

Pons Sublicius

Cloaca Maxima

Porta
Querquetulana

Pons Aemilius

Circus Maximus

PALATINE HILL

Porta
Trigemina

CAELIAN HILL

Porta
Caelimontana

AVENTINE   HILL

VIA PORTUENSIS

Emporium

Porta
Lavernalis

VIA LATINA

Tiber

VIA OSTIENSIS

VIA APPIA

In the first century BC first Sulla and
then Caesar undertook enormous
building operations.

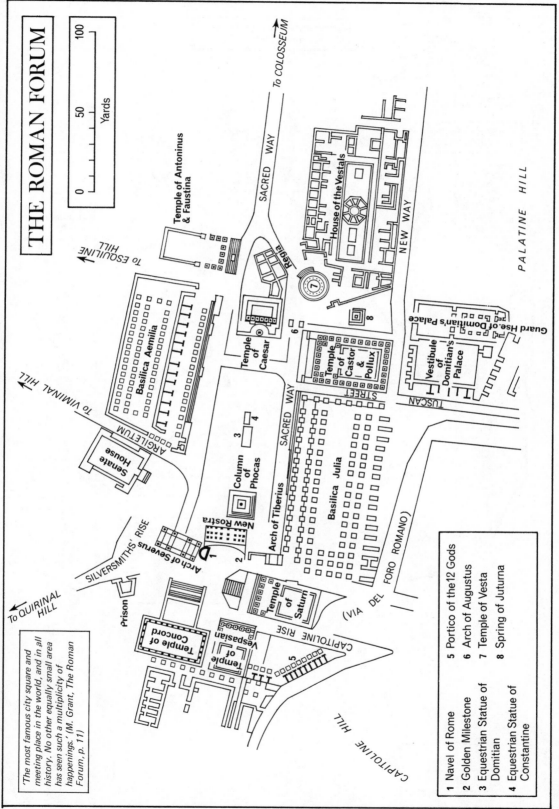

THE ROMAN FORUM

Yards
0   50   100

'The most famous city square and meeting place in the world, and in all history. No other equally small area has seen such a multiplicity of happenings.' (M. Grant, The Roman Forum, p. 11)

To ESQUILINE HILL

Temple of Antoninus & Faustina

Basilica Aemilia

To VIMINAL HILL

ARGILETUM

Senate House

SILVERSMITHS' RISE

To QUIRINAL HILL

Prison

Temple of Concord

Temple of Vespasian

CAPITOLINE RISE

Temple of Saturn

Column of Phocas

New Rostra

Arch of Tiberius

Arch of Severus

3
4

2
1

5

Temple of Caesar

SACRED WAY

Regia

7

8

6

House of the Vestals

SACRED WAY

Temple of Castor & Pollux

STREET

SACRED WAY

Basilica Julia

(VIA DEL FORO ROMANO)

TUSCAN

NEW WAY

Vestibule of Domitian's Palace

Guard Hse. of Domitian's Palace

PALATINE HILL

To COLOSSEUM

CAPITOLINE HILL

1 Navel of Rome
2 Golden Milestone
3 Equestrian Statue of Domitian
4 Equestrian Statue of Constantine

5 Portico of the 12 Gods
6 Arch of Augustus
7 Temple of Vesta
8 Spring of Juturna

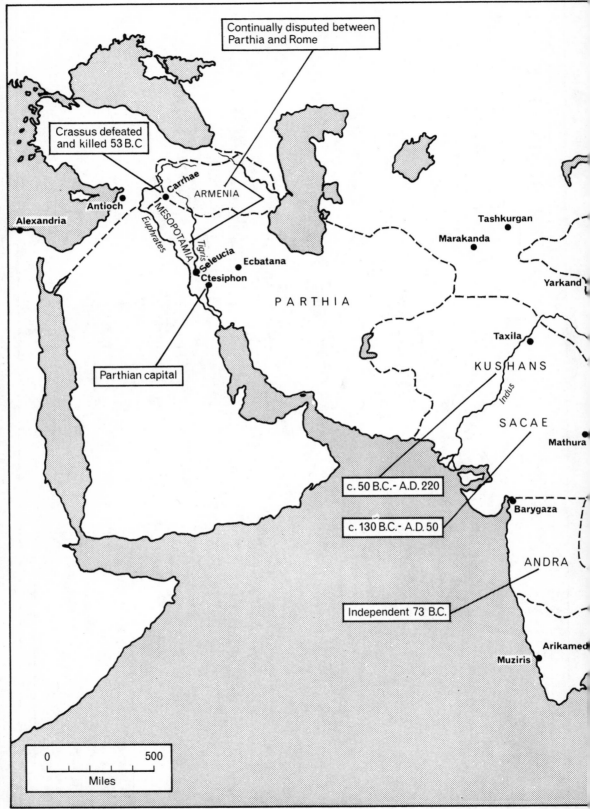

Continually disputed between
Parthia and Rome

Crassus defeated
and killed 53 B.C

Parthian capital

Alexandria

Antioch

Carrhae

ARMENIA

MESOPOTAMIA

Euphrates

Tigris

Seleucia

Ctesiphon

Ecbatana

PARTHIA

Tashkurgan

Marakanda

Yarkand

Taxila

KUSHANS

Indus

SACAE

Mathura

c. 50 B.C.- A.D. 220

c. 130 B.C.- A.D. 50

Barygaza

ANDRA

Independent 73 B.C.

Arikamed

Muziris

0   500

Miles

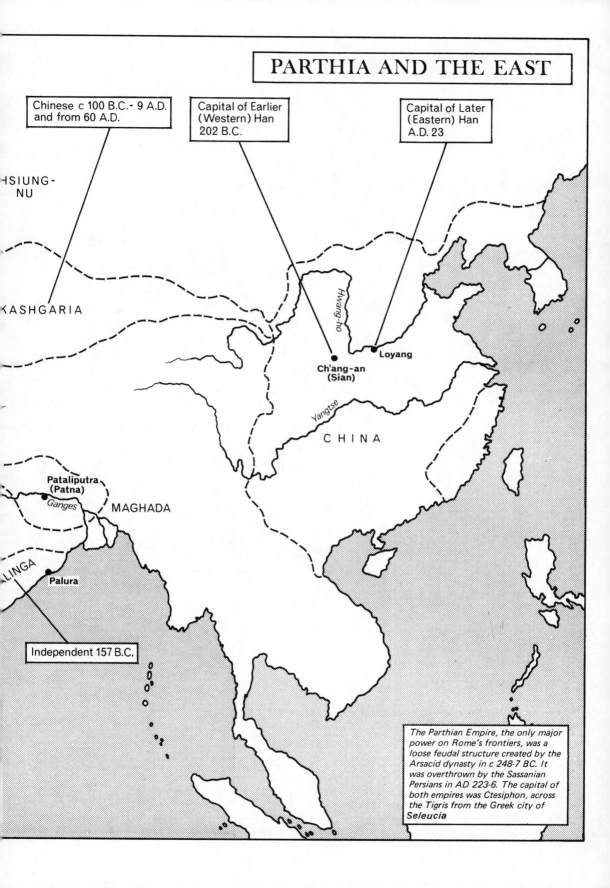

PARTHIA AND THE EAST

Chinese c 100 B.C.- 9 A.D. and from 60 A.D.

Capital of Earlier (Western) Han 202 B.C.

Capital of Later (Eastern) Han A.D. 23

HSIUNG-NU

KASHGARIA

Hwang-ho

Loyang

Ch'ang-an (Sian)

Yangtse

C H I N A

Pataliputra (Patna)

Ganges

MAGHADA

LINGA

Palura

Independent 157 B.C.

The Parthian Empire, the only major power on Rome's frontiers, was a loose feudal structure created by the Arsacid dynasty in c 248-7 BC. It was overthrown by the Sassanian Persians in AD 223-6. The capital of both empires was Ctesiphon, across the Tigris from the Greek city of **Seleucia**

FREE GERMANY

Temporarily conquered from 15 B.C. but abandoned after ambushing of Varus by Arminius in A.D. 9

BRITANNIA

LWR. GERMANY (17 B.C.)

Colonia Agrippinensis

Moguntiacum

LOWER PANNONIA (10 B.C.)

BELGICA

LUGDUNENSIS

RHAETIA (15 B.C.)

NORICUM (15 B.C.)

UPPER PANNONIA

UPR. GERMANY (17 B.C.)

Aquileia

Lugdunum

AQUITANIA

P

C

M

NARBONENSIS

Nemausus

I T A L Y

Adriatic Sea

Rome

TARRACONENSIS

LUSITANIA (c. 27 B.C.)

Tarraco

Naulochus

Corduba

BAETICA

SICILY

Gades

Carthage

Naval victory over Sextus Pompeius 36 B.C.

M A U R E T A N I A

A F R I C A

—————— Imperial frontier as in A.D. 14

– – – – – Provincial frontiers

ASIA Senatorial provinces

ALPINE PROVINCES (15-14 B.C.)
M: Maritime, C: Cottian, P: Pennine

The hatched areas represent the more important dependent ('client') states, whose monarchs enjoyed internal autonomy but had to support Rome's foreign policy and help defend the imperial frontiers.

////// Principal client states

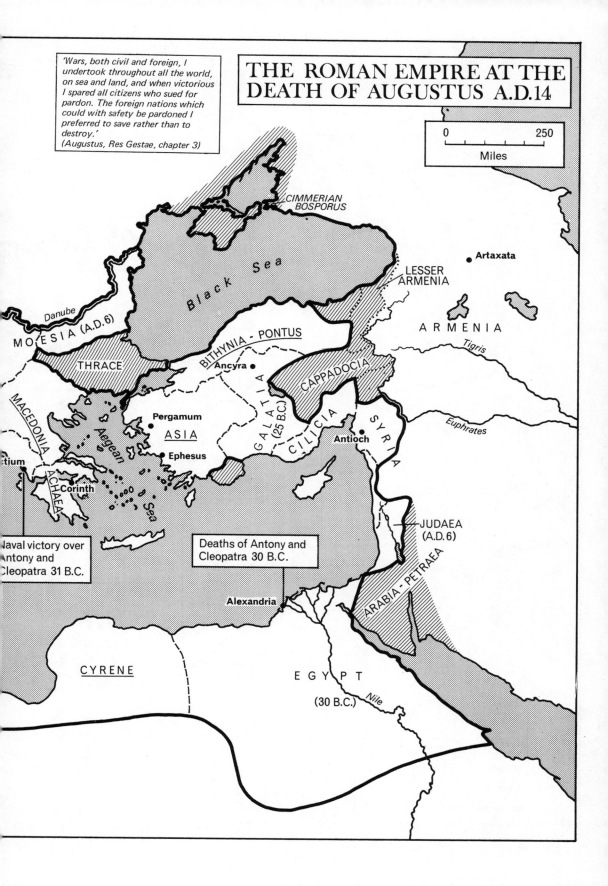

'Wars, both civil and foreign, I
undertook throughout all the world,
on sea and land, and when victorious
I spared all citizens who sued for
pardon. The foreign nations which
could with safety be pardoned I
preferred to save rather than to
destroy.'
(Augustus, Res Gestae, chapter 3)

THE ROMAN EMPIRE AT THE
DEATH OF AUGUSTUS A.D.14

0   250

Miles

CIMMERIAN
BOSPORUS

Artaxata

LESSER
ARMENIA

Black Sea

A R M E N I A

Danube

Tigris

MOESIA (A.D.6)

BITHYNIA - PONTUS

THRACE

Ancyra

CAPPADOCIA

MACEDONIA

Pergamum

ASIA

Ephesus

G
A
L
A
T
I
A
(25 B.C.)

CILICIA

SYRIA

Antioch

Euphrates

Aegean Sea

ACHAEA

Corinth

tium

Naval victory over
Antony and
Cleopatra 31 B.C.

Deaths of Antony and
Cleopatra 30 B.C.

JUDAEA
(A.D.6)

ARABIA - PETRAEA

Alexandria

CYRENE

E G Y P T

(30 B.C.)

Nile

GAUL

Rhine

Danube

Rhone

Arelate

Narbo

VIA DOMITIA

Forum
Julii

Rome

Ebro

SPAIN

Adriatic
Sea

Tyrrhenian
Sea

Mediterranean

AFRICA

Imperial frontier as in A.D.14

Roman roads

Mountain contours

All roads lead to Rome: the most
potent guarantees of external and
internal peace and stimulants of
prosperity.

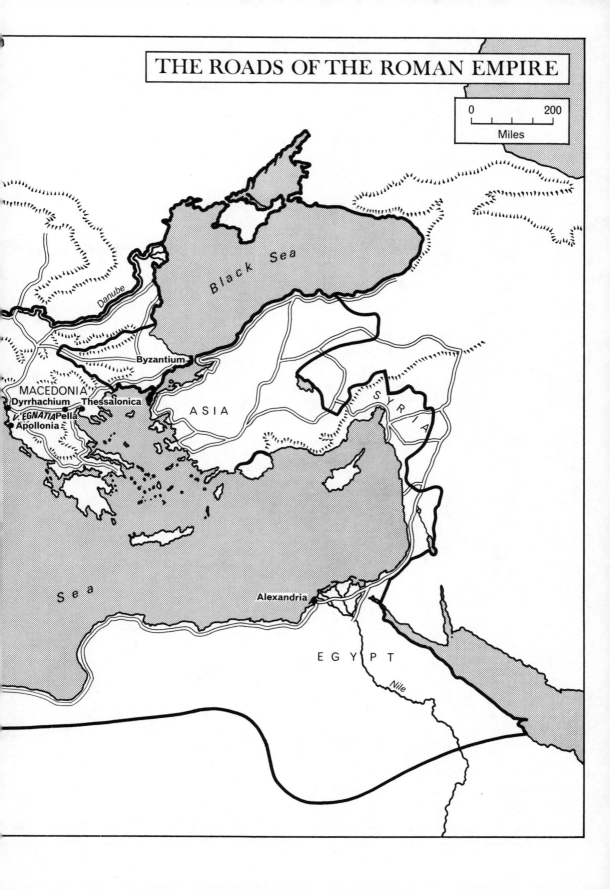

THE ROADS OF THE ROMAN EMPIRE

0 ___ 200
Miles

Black Sea

Danube

Byzantium

MACEDONIA
Dyrrhachium   Thessalonica
V. EGNATIA Pella
Apollonia

ASIA

S Y R I A

Sea

Alexandria

E G Y P T

Nile

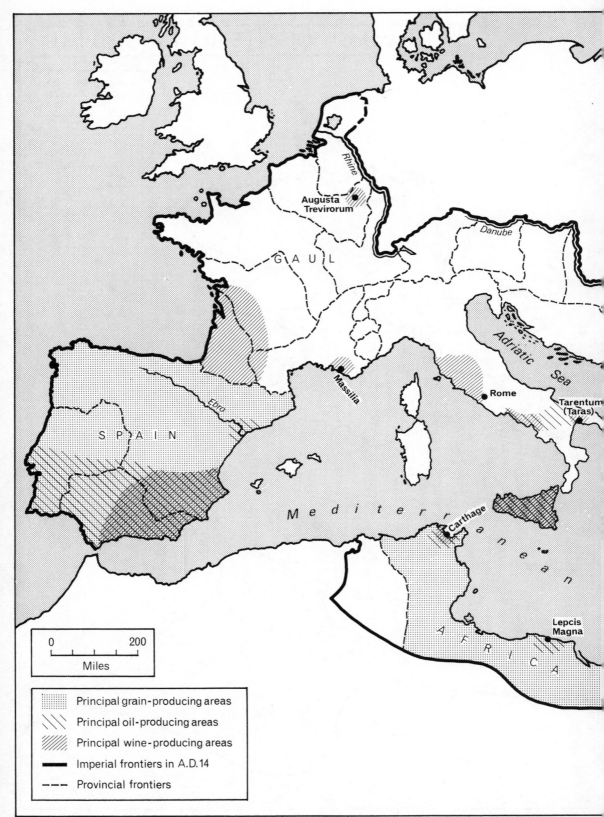

Augusta
Trevirorum

Rhine

Danube

G A U L

Ebro

S P A I N

Massilia

Rome

Adriatic

Sea

Tarentum
(Taras)

M e d i t e r r a n e a n

Carthage

A F R I C A

Lepcis
Magna

0		200

Miles

Principal grain-producing areas

Principal oil-producing areas

Principal wine-producing areas

Imperial frontiers in A.D. 14

Provincial frontiers

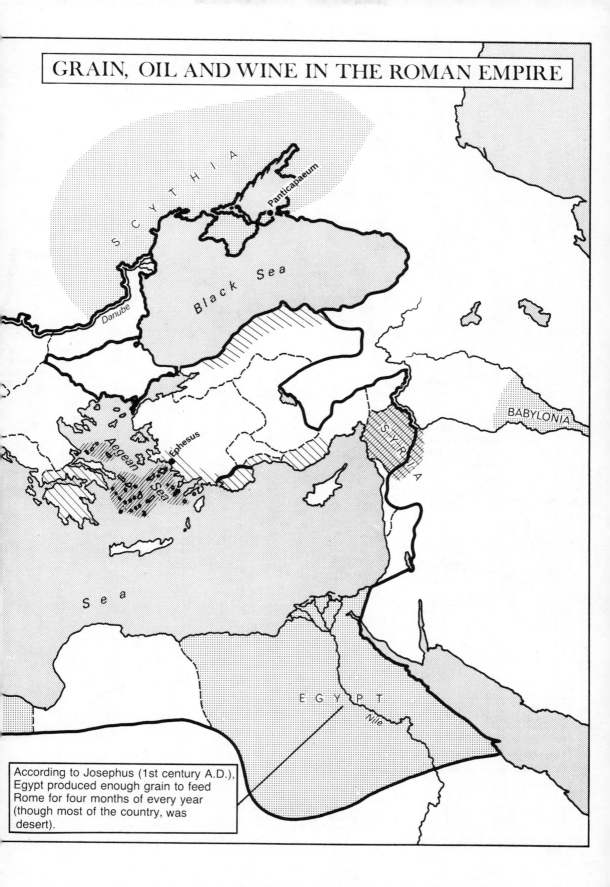

GRAIN, OIL AND WINE IN THE ROMAN EMPIRE

SCYTHIA

Panticapaeum

Black Sea

Danube

BABYLONIA

SYRIA

Aegean

Ephesus

Sea

Sea

EGYPT

Nile

According to Josephus (1st century A.D.),
Egypt produced enough grain to feed
Rome for four months of every year
(though most of the country, was
desert).

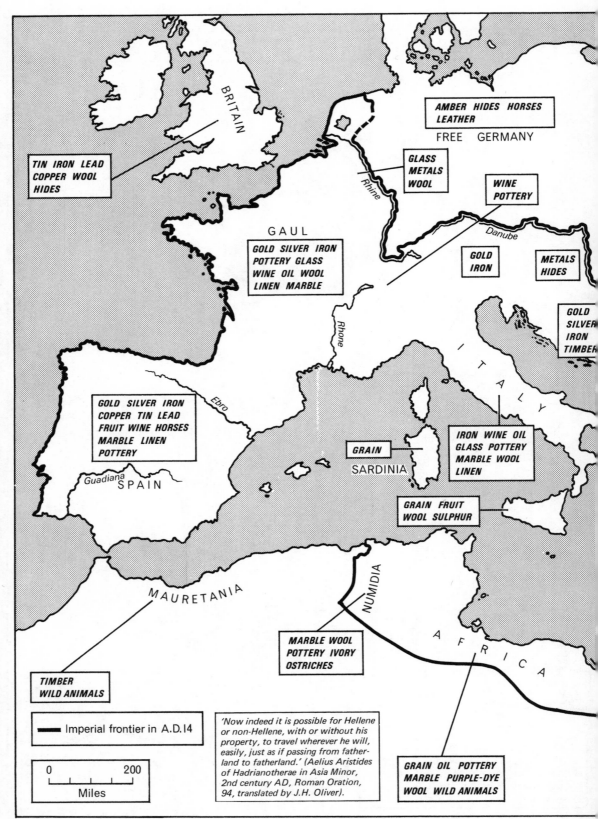

BRITAIN

TIN IRON LEAD
COPPER WOOL
HIDES

FREE GERMANY

AMBER HIDES HORSES
LEATHER

GLASS
METALS
WOOL

Rhine

WINE
POTTERY

GAUL

GOLD SILVER IRON
POTTERY GLASS
WINE OIL WOOL
LINEN MARBLE

Danube

GOLD
IRON

METALS
HIDES

Rhone

GOLD
SILVER
IRON
TIMBER

I T A L Y

Ebro

GOLD SILVER IRON
COPPER TIN LEAD
FRUIT WINE HORSES
MARBLE LINEN
POTTERY

GRAIN

SARDINIA

IRON WINE OIL
GLASS POTTERY
MARBLE WOOL
LINEN

Guadiana SPAIN

GRAIN FRUIT
WOOL SULPHUR

MAURETANIA

NUMIDIA

A F R I C A

MARBLE WOOL
POTTERY IVORY
OSTRICHES

TIMBER
WILD ANIMALS

—— Imperial frontier in A.D.14

0   200
Miles

'Now indeed it is possible for Hellene
or non-Hellene, with or without his
property, to travel wherever he will,
easily, just as if passing from fatherland to fatherland.' (Aelius Aristides
of Hadrianotherae in Asia Minor,
2nd century AD, Roman Oration,
94, translated by J.H. Oliver).

GRAIN OIL POTTERY
MARBLE PURPLE-DYE
WOOL WILD ANIMALS

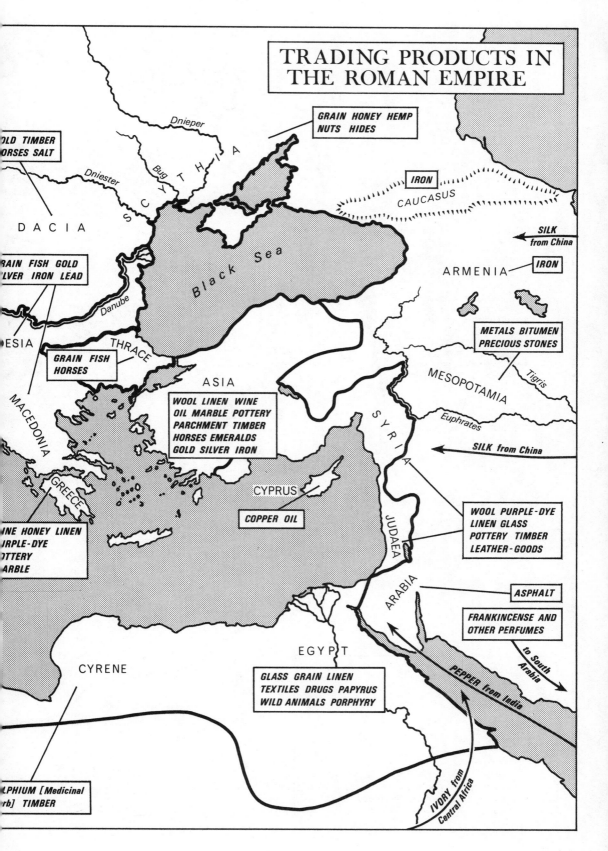

TRADING PRODUCTS IN THE ROMAN EMPIRE

Dnieper

GRAIN HONEY HEMP
NUTS HIDES

OLD TIMBER
ORSES SALT

Dniester

IRON

CAUCASUS

SILK
from China

S C Y T H I A

Bug

DACIA

ARMENIA

IRON

RAIN FISH GOLD
LVER IRON LEAD

Danube

Black Sea

METALS BITUMEN
PRECIOUS STONES

ESIA

THRACE

GRAIN FISH
HORSES

MESOPOTAMIA

Tigris

ASIA

MACEDONIA

WOOL LINEN WINE
OIL MARBLE POTTERY
PARCHMENT TIMBER
HORSES EMERALDS
GOLD SILVER IRON

S
Y
R
I
A

Euphrates

SILK from China

GREECE

CYPRUS

COPPER OIL

J
U
D
A
E
A

WOOL PURPLE-DYE
LINEN GLASS
POTTERY TIMBER
LEATHER-GOODS

NE HONEY LINEN
URPLE-DYE
OTTERY
ARBLE

A
R
A
B
I
A

ASPHALT

FRANKINCENSE AND
OTHER PERFUMES

to South
Arabia

EGYPT

CYRENE

GLASS GRAIN LINEN
TEXTILES DRUGS PAPYRUS
WILD ANIMALS PORPHYRY

PEPPER from India

LPHIUM [Medicinal
rb] TIMBER

IVORY from
Central Africa

F

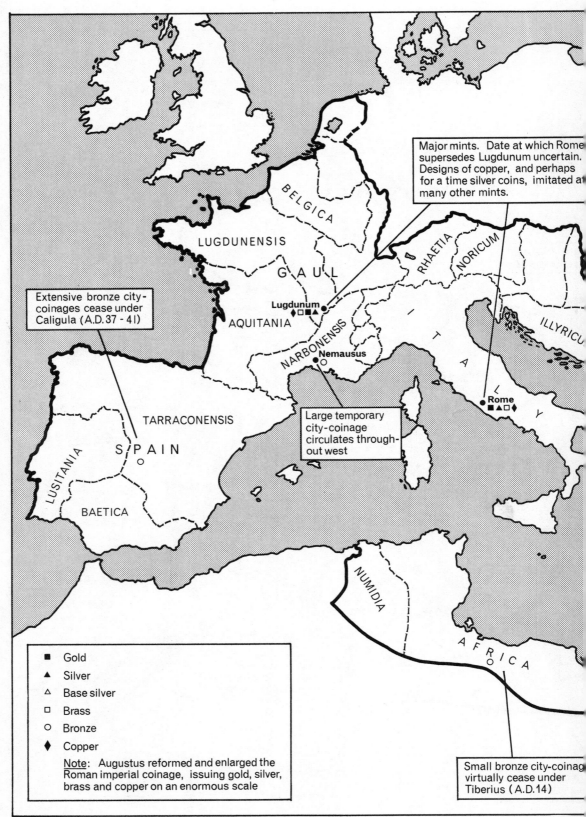

Major mints. Date at which Rome supersedes Lugdunum uncertain. Designs of copper, and perhaps for a time silver coins, imitated at many other mints.

Extensive bronze city-coinages cease under Caligula (A.D. 37 - 41)

Large temporary city-coinage circulates throughout west

BELGICA

LUGDUNENSIS

GAUL

AQUITANIA

Lugdunum ◆ □ ■ ▲

NARBONENSIS

Nemausus ○

RHAETIA

NORICUM

ILLYRICU

I
T
A
L
Y

Rome ■ ▲ □ ◆

TARRACONENSIS

S P A I N ○

LUSITANIA

BAETICA

NUMIDIA

A F R I C A ○

Small bronze city-coinag virtually cease under Tiberius (A.D.14)

■ Gold
▲ Silver
△ Base silver
□ Brass
○ Bronze
◆ Copper

Note: Augustus reformed and enlarged the Roman imperial coinage, issuing gold, silver, brass and copper on an enormous scale

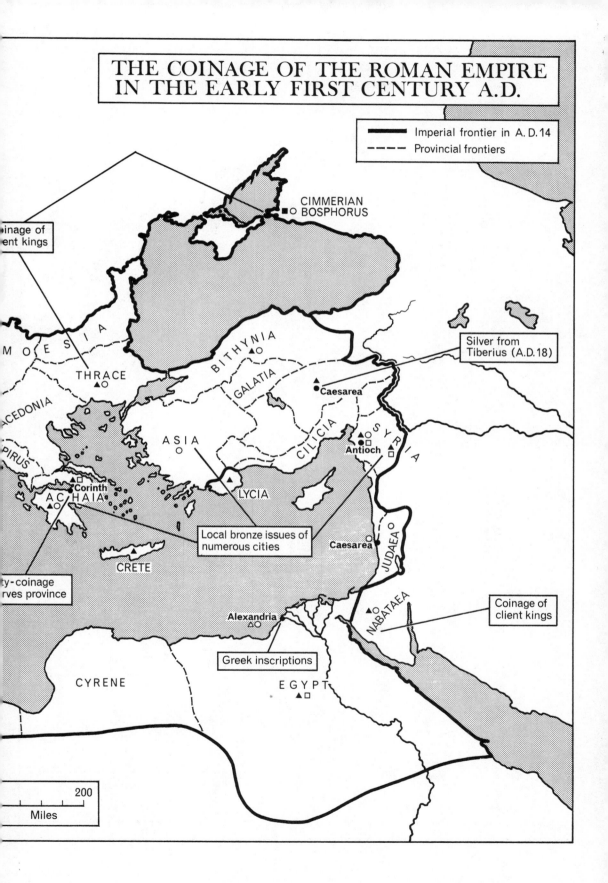

THE COINAGE OF THE ROMAN EMPIRE
IN THE EARLY FIRST CENTURY A.D.

—— Imperial frontier in A.D.14
--- Provincial frontiers

CIMMERIAN
■ O BOSPHORUS

...inage of
...ent kings

M O E S I A

THRACE
▲ O

ACEDONIA

PIRUS

ASIA
O

A C H A I A
▲ O

Corinth
▲ □

CRETE

...ty-coinage
...rves province

CYRENE

BITHYNIA
▲ O

GALATIA

▲
● Caesarea

C I L I C I A

S Y R I A

▲ O
● □
Antioch

Silver from
Tiberius (A.D.18)

LYCIA
▲

Local bronze issues of
numerous cities

Caesarea
O

JUDAEA O

NABATAEA
▲ O

Coinage of
client kings

Alexandria
△ O

Greek inscriptions

E G Y P T
▲ □

200
Miles

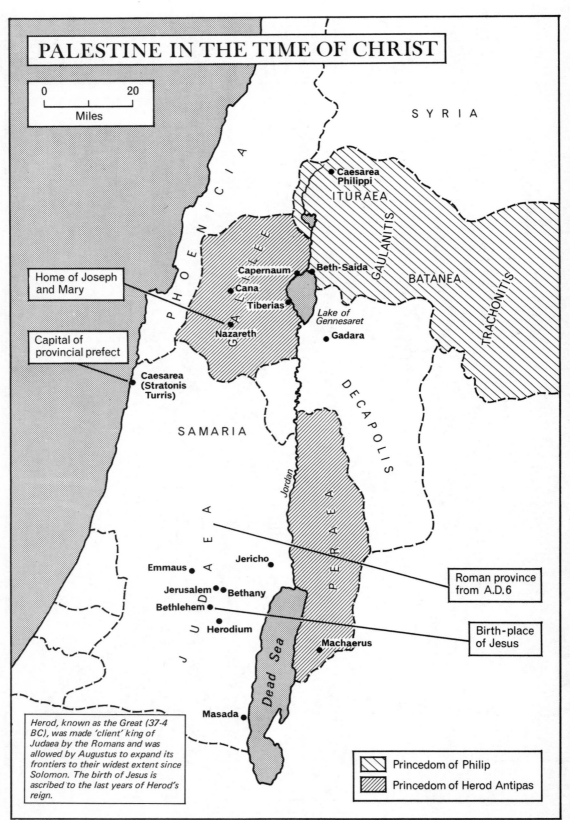

PALESTINE IN THE TIME OF CHRIST

0 20
Miles

SYRIA

Caesarea
Philippi

ITURAEA

GAULANITIS

BATANEA

TRACHONITIS

PHOENICIA

GALILEE

Home of Joseph
and Mary

Capernaum
Cana
Tiberias

Beth-Saida

Lake of
Gennesaret

Nazareth

Gadara

Capital of
provincial prefect

Caesarea
(Stratonis
Turris)

SAMARIA

DECAPOLIS

Jordan

PERAEA

Emmaus

Jericho

Jerusalem
Bethany
Bethlehem

J U D A E A

Herodium

Roman province
from A.D.6

Machaerus

Birth-place
of Jesus

Dead Sea

Masada

*Herod, known as the Great (37-4
BC), was made 'client' king of
Judaea by the Romans and was
allowed by Augustus to expand its
frontiers to their widest extent since
Solomon. The birth of Jesus is
ascribed to the last years of Herod's
reign.*

/// Princedom of Philip

/// Princedom of Herod Antipas

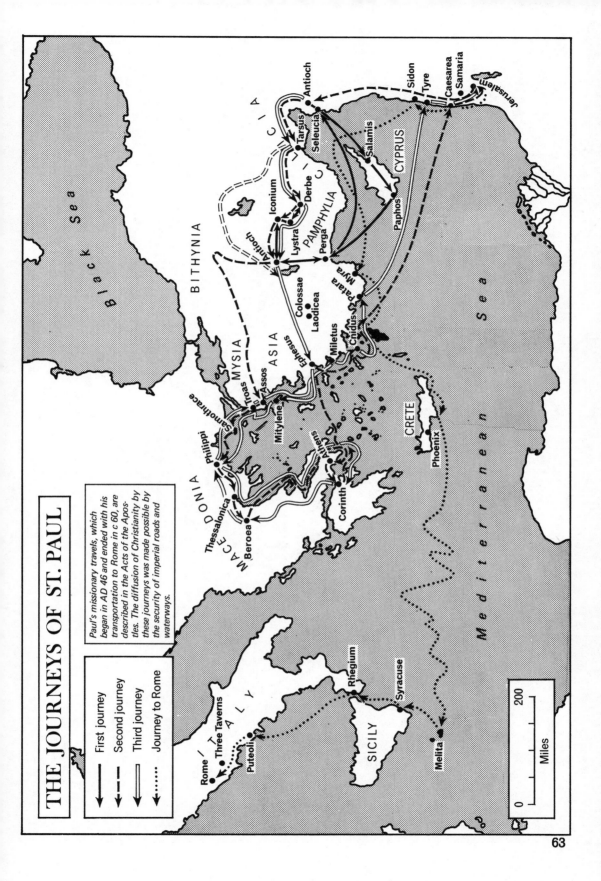

THE JOURNEYS OF ST. PAUL

Paul's missionary travels, which began in AD 46 and ended with his transportation to Rome in c 60, are described in the Acts of the Apostles. The diffusion of Christianity by these journeys was made possible by the security of imperial roads and waterways.

First journey
Second journey
Third journey
Journey to Rome

Black Sea

BITHYNIA

MYSIA

ASIA

MACEDONIA

CRETE

Mediterranean Sea

ITALY

SICILY

Rome
Three Taverns
Puteoli
Rhegium
Syracuse
Melita

Thessalonica
Beroea
Philippi
Athens
Corinth
Samothrace
Troas
Assos
Mitylene
Ephesus
Miletus
Cnidus
Phoenix

Colossae
Laodicea
Patara
Myra
Perga
PAMPHYLIA
Lystra
Derbe
Iconium
Antioch

Tarsus
Seleucia
Antioch
CILICIA
Salamis
CYPRUS
Paphos

Sidon
Tyre
Caesarea
Samaria
Jerusalem

200

0   Miles

63

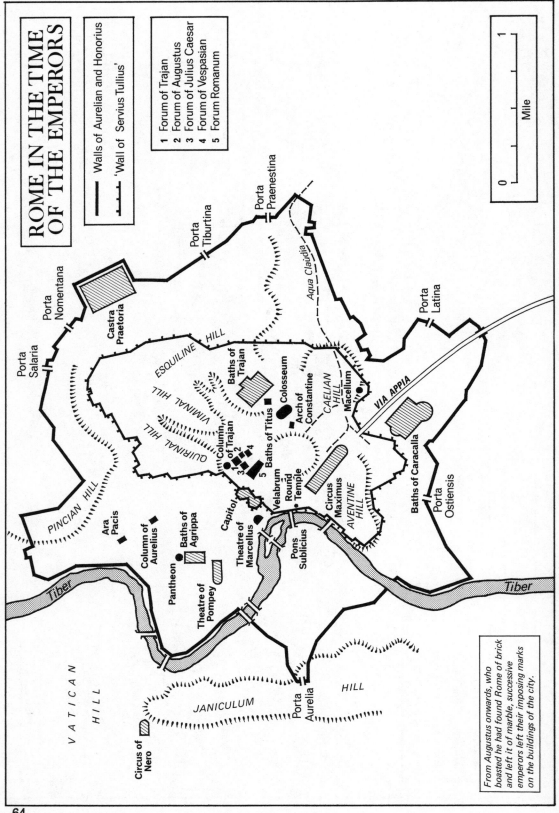

ROME IN THE TIME OF THE EMPERORS

Walls of Aurelian and Honorius
'Wall of Servius Tullius'

1 Forum of Trajan
2 Forum of Augustus
3 Forum of Julius Caesar
4 Forum of Vespasian
5 Forum Romanum

0   1
Mile

Porta Tiburtina

Porta Praenestina

Aqua Claudia

Porta Latina

Porta Nomentana

Castra Praetoria

Porta Salaria

ESQUILINE HILL

Baths of Trajan

Colosseum

CAELIAN HILL

Macellum

VIMINAL HILL

Arch of Constantine

VIA APPIA

QUIRINAL HILL

Column of Trajan

Baths of Titus

PINCIAN HILL

2
3   4
1
5

Velabrum
Round Temple

Circus Maximus

Baths of Caracalla

Ara Pacis

Capitol

AVENTINE HILL

Porta Ostiensis

Column of Aurelius

Baths of Agrippa

Theatre of Marcellus

Pantheon

Theatre of Pompey

Pons Sublicius

Tiber

Tiber

VATICAN HILL

JANICULUM HILL

Porta Aurelia

Circus of Nero

From Augustus onwards, who boasted he had found Rome of brick and left it of marble, successive emperors left their imposing marks on the buildings of the city.

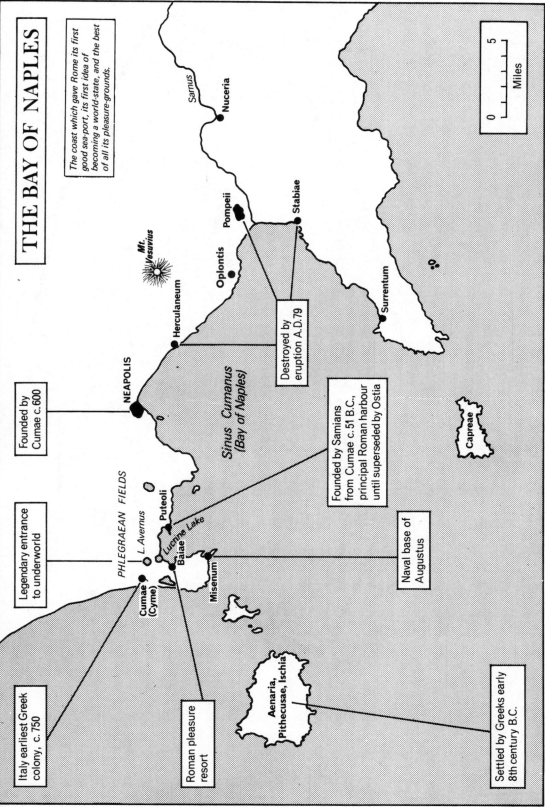

THE BAY OF NAPLES

The coast which gave Rome its first good sea-port, its first idea of becoming a world-state, and the best of all its pleasure-grounds.

Founded by Cumae c.600

Legendary entrance to underworld

Italy earliest Greek colony, c. 750

Roman pleasure resort

Naval base of Augustus

Founded by Samians from Cumae c.51 B.C., principal Roman harbour until superseded by Ostia

Destroyed by eruption A.D.79

Settled by Greeks early 8th century B.C.

Sarnus

Nuceria

Mt. Vesuvius

Pompeii

Stabiae

Oplontis

Surrentum

Herculaneum

NEAPOLIS

Sinus Cumanus (Bay of Naples)

PHLEGRAEAN FIELDS

Puteoli

L. Avernus

Lucrine Lake

Baiae

Misenum

Cumae (Cyme)

Capreae

Aenaria, Pithecusae, Ischia

0 5
Miles

65

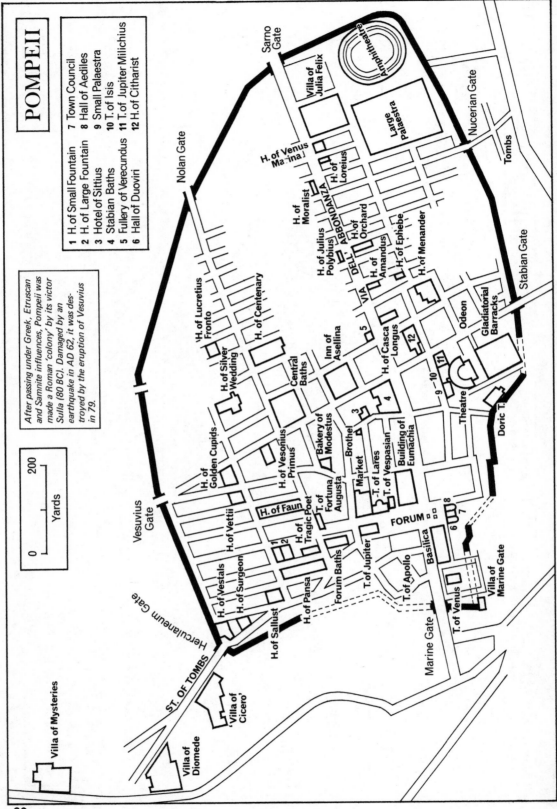

POMPEII

1 H. of Small Fountain
2 H. of Large Fountain
3 Hotel of Sittius
4 Stabian Baths
5 Fullery of Verecundus
6 Hall of Duoviri
7 Town Council
8 Hall of Aediles
9 Small Palaestra
10 T. of Isis
11 T. of Jupiter Milichius
12 H. of Citharist

After passing under Greek, Etruscan and Samnite influences, Pompeii was made a Roman 'colony' by its victor Sulla (80 BC). Damaged by an earthquake in AD 62, it was destroyed by the eruption of Vesuvius in 79.

0   200
Yards

Sarno Gate

Villa of Julia Felix

Amphitheatre

Large Palaestra

Nucerian Gate

Tombs

H. of Venus Marina

H. of Loreius

Stabian Gate

Nolan Gate

H. of Moralist

DELL' ABBONDANZA

H. of Orchard

H. of Julius Polybius

VIA

H. of Amandus

H. of Ephebe

H. of Menander

H. of Lucretius Fronto

H. of Centenary

Inn of Asellina

H. of Casca Longus

Odeon

Gladiatorial Barracks

H. of Silver Wedding

Central Baths

5

12

9–10
11

H. of Golden Cupids

Bakery of Modestus

Brothel

4

Theatre

Doric T.

H. of Vesonius Primus

T. of Fortuna Augusta

Market

3

T. of Lares

T. of Vespasian

Building of Eumachia

H. of Faun

FORUM

Vesuvius Gate

H. of Vettii

H. of Tragic Poet

1
2

Forum Baths

T. of Jupiter

Basilica

8
7

6

H. of Vestals

H. of Surgeon

H. of Pansa

T. of Apollo

T. of Venus

Villa of Marine Gate

Herculaneum Gate

H. of Sallust

Marine Gate

ST. OF TOMBS

Villa of Mysteries

'Villa of Cicero'

Villa of Diomede

66

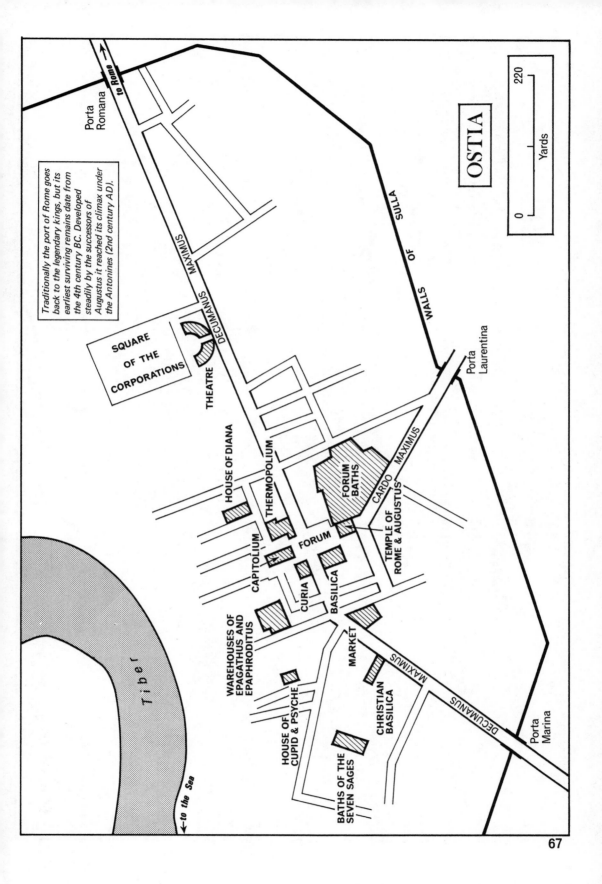

OSTIA

0   220

Yards

Traditionally the port of Rome goes back to the legendary kings, but its earliest surviving remains date from the 4th century BC. Developed steadily by the successors of Augustus it reached its climax under the Antonines (2nd century AD).

Porta Romana

to Rome

SQUARE OF THE CORPORATIONS

THEATRE

DECUMANUS MAXIMUS

WALLS OF SULLA

Porta Laurentina

HOUSE OF DIANA

THERMOPOLIUM

CAPITOLIUM

FORUM

FORUM BATHS

CARDO MAXIMUS

CURIA

BASILICA

TEMPLE OF ROME & AUGUSTUS

WAREHOUSES OF EPAGATHUS AND EPAPHRODITUS

HOUSE OF CUPID & PSYCHE

MARKET

CHRISTIAN BASILICA

DECUMANUS MAXIMUS

Porta Marina

BATHS OF THE SEVEN SAGES

Tiber

to the Sea

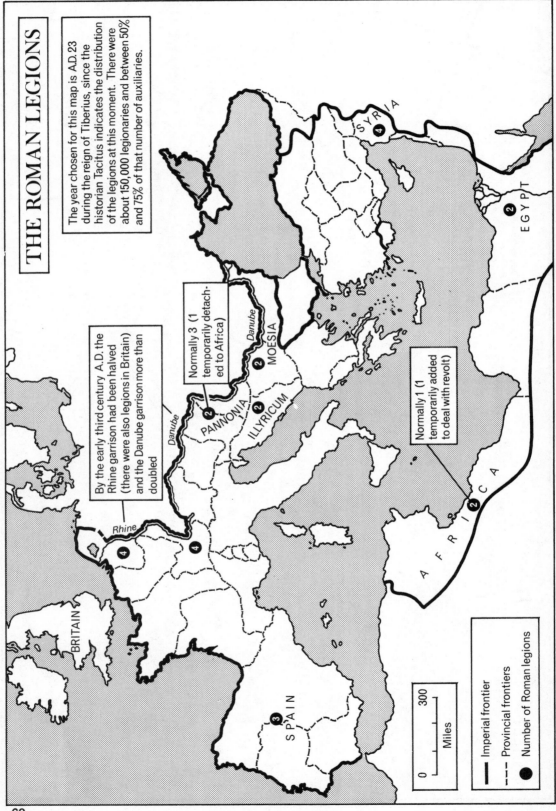

THE ROMAN LEGIONS

The year chosen for this map is A.D. 23 during the reign of Tiberius, since the historian Tacitus indicates the distribution of the legions at this moment. There were about 150,000 legionaries and between 50% and 75% of that number of auxiliaries.

Normally 3 (1 temporarily detached to Africa)

Normally 1 (1 temporarily added to deal with revolt)

By the early third century A.D. the Rhine garrison had been halved (there were also legions in Britain) and the Danube garrison more than doubled

SYRIA ④

EGYPT ②

Danube

MOESIA ②

PANNONIA ② ② ILLYRICUM

AFRICA ②

Danube

Rhine

BRITAIN

④ ④

SPAIN ③

0	300

Miles

—— Imperial frontier

- - - Provincial frontiers

● Number of Roman legions

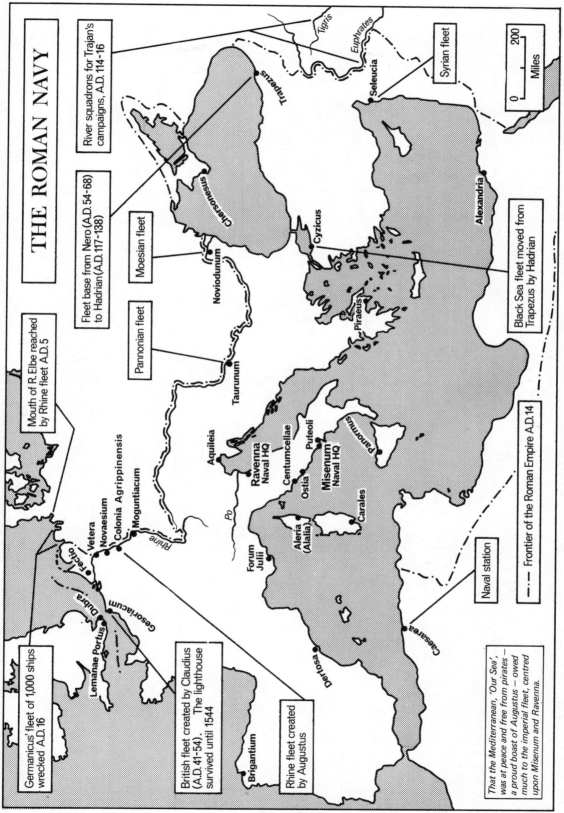

THE ROMAN NAVY

River squadrons for Trajan's campaigns, A.D. 114-16

Syrian fleet

200 Miles

Fleet base from Nero (A.D. 54-68) to Hadrian (A.D. 117-138)

Moesian fleet

Pannonian fleet

Black Sea fleet moved from Trapezus by Hadrian

Mouth of R. Elbe reached by Rhine fleet A.D. 5

Germanicus' fleet of 1,000 ships wrecked A.D. 16

British fleet created by Claudius (A.D. 41-54). The lighthouse survived until 1544

Rhine fleet created by Augustus

Naval station

Frontier of the Roman Empire A.D. 14

That the Mediterranean, 'Our Sea', was at peace and free from pirates — a proud boast of Augustus — owed much to the imperial fleet, centred upon Misenum and Ravenna.

Tigris

Euphrates

Seleucia

Trapezus

Alexandria

Chersonesus

Cyzicus

Noviodunum

Piraeus

Taurunum

Aquileia

Ravenna Naval HQ

Centumcellae

Puteoli

Ostia

Misenum Naval HQ

Panormus

Carales

Forum Julii

Aleria (Alalia)

Caesarea

Dertosa

Po

Rhine

Moguntiacum

Colonia Agrippinensis

Novaesium

Vetera

Fectio

Gesoriacum

Dubra

Lemanae Portus

Brigantium

69

BRITANNIA (AD 71)
(AD 59)
(AD 43-47)
Londinium

FREE GERMANY

LOWER
GERMANY
Colonia Agrippinensis

Moguntiacum

Rhine

AGRI
DECUMAT
(83)

RHAETIA

NORICUM

PANNONIA

Danube

UPPER

LOWER

ILLYRICUM

LUGDUNENSIS

UPPER GERMANY

G A L L I A

Lugdunum

AQUITANIA

NARBONENSIS

Nemausus

Aquileia

I T A L I A

Adriatic Sea

TARRACONENSIS

Tarraco

H I S P A N I A

LUSITANIA

SARDINIA

BAETICA

Corduba

Gades

Rome

SICILY

Carthage

MAURETANIA (A.D.42)

A F R I C A

- – – Frontier of Roman Empire A.D.14
- ·– · Frontier of Roman Empire A.D.117
······· Province boundaries

THE ROMAN EMPIRE FROM TIBERIUS (A.D.14-37) TO TRAJAN (98-117)

Trajan's expansion as far as the Persian Gulf came to nothing, since his successor Hadrian withdrew to the Euphrates again.

KINGDOM OF BOSPHORUS

Black Sea

Artaxata

SIA

THRACIA
(A.D.44)

BITHYNIA - PONTUS

ARMENIA MINOR
(63)

ARMENIA
(A.D.114)

ASSYRIA
(AD.115)

Ancyra

Pergamum

ASIA

GALATIA

CAPPADOCIA
(A.D.17)

MESOPOTAMIA
(A.D.115)

Tigris

Corinth

Ephesus

PAMPHYLIA
(43)

LYCIA

Aegean Sea

Antioch

SYRIA

Euphrates

JUDAEA
(A.D.6,44)

Regions beyond Euphrates
evacuated by Hadrian A.D.117

Alexandria

ARABIA
(A.D.106)

CYRENE

EGYPT

Nile

0	200

Miles

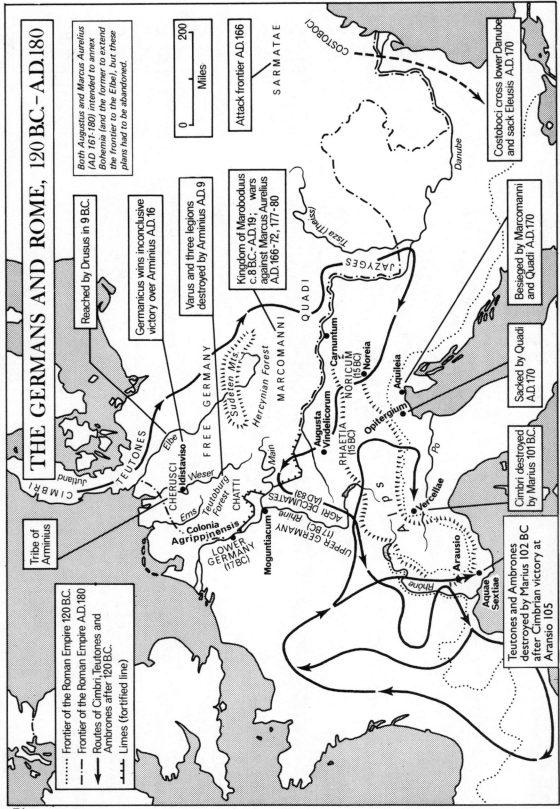

THE GERMANS AND ROME, 120 B.C.–A.D.180

Both Augustus and Marcus Aurelius (AD 161-180) intended to annex Bohemia (and the former to extend the frontier to the Elbe), but these plans had to be abandoned.

200

Miles

0

Attack frontier A.D.166

Costoboci cross lower Danube and sack Eleusis A.D.170

Besieged by Marcomanni and Quadi A.D.170

Sacked by Quadi A.D.170

Cimbri destroyed by Marius 101 B.C.

Teutones and Ambrones destroyed by Marius 102 BC after Cimbrian victory at Aransio 105

Kingdom of Maroboduus c.8 B.C.-A.D.19; wars against Marcus Aurelius A.D.166-72, 177-80

Varus and three legions destroyed by Arminius A.D.9

Germanicus wins inconclusive victory over Arminius A.D.16

Reached by Drusus in 9 B.C.

Tribe of Arminius

Frontier of the Roman Empire 120 B.C.
Frontier of the Roman Empire A.D.180
Routes of Cimbri, Teutones and Ambrones after 120 B.C.
Limes (fortified line)

SARMATAE

COSTOBOCI

Danube

Tisza (Theiss)

JAZYGES

QUADI

MARCOMANNI

FREE GERMANY

Sudeten Mts.

Hercynian Forest

TEUTONES

CIMBRI

Jutland

Elbe

CHERUSCI

Idistaviso

Weser

Ems

Teutoburg Forest

CHATTI

Main

Rhine

Colonia Agrippinensis

LOWER GERMANY (17BC)

Moguntiacum

AGRI DECUMATES (AD 83)

UPPER GERMANY (17BC)

Augusta Vindelicorum

RHAETIA (15BC)

NORICUM (15BC)

Carnuntum

Noreia

Aquileia

Opitergium

A L P S

Po

Vercellae

Arausio

Rhone

Aquae Sextiae

71

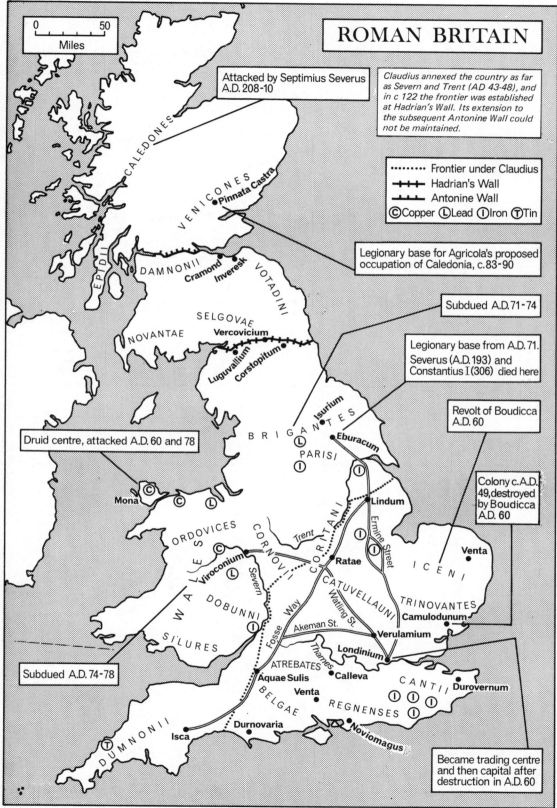

ROMAN BRITAIN

Attacked by Septimius Severus A.D. 208-10

Claudius annexed the country as far as Severn and Trent (AD 43-48), and in c 122 the frontier was established at Hadrian's Wall. Its extension to the subsequent Antonine Wall could not be maintained.

.... Frontier under Claudius
┼┼┼┼ Hadrian's Wall
┴┴┴┴ Antonine Wall
ⒸCopper ⓁLead ⒾIron ⓉTin

Legionary base for Agricola's proposed occupation of Caledonia, c.83-90

Subdued A.D. 71-74

Legionary base from A.D. 71. Severus (A.D. 193) and Constantius I (306) died here

Revolt of Boudicca A.D. 60

Druid centre, attacked A.D. 60 and 78

Colony c.A.D. 49, destroyed by Boudicca A.D. 60

Subdued A.D. 74-78

Became trading centre and then capital after destruction in A.D. 60

0   50
Miles

CALEDONES

VENICONES

Pinnata Castra

EPIDII

DAMNONII

Cramond

Inveresk

VOTADINI

SELGOVAE

Vercovicium

NOVANTAE

Luguvalium   Corstopitum

Isurium

BRIGANTES

Eburacum

PARISI

Ⓛ

Ⓘ

Mona

Ⓒ

Ⓒ   Ⓛ

Ⓘ

ORDOVICES

CORNOVII

Ⓒ

Viroconium

Ⓛ

Lindum

Trent

Ⓘ

CORITANI

Ernine Street

Ⓘ

Ⓘ

Ratae

Venta

ICENI

W A L E S

Severn

DOBUNNI

Ⓘ

CATUVELLAUNI

TRINOVANTES

SILURES

Fosse Way

Akeman St.

Watling St.

Camulodunum

Verulamium

Thames

Londinium

ATREBATES

Calleva

CANTII

Durovernum

Aquae Sulis

Venta

BELGAE

REGNESES

Ⓘ   Ⓘ   Ⓘ

Ⓘ   Ⓘ

DUMNONII

Ⓣ

Isca

Durnovaria

Noviomagus

72

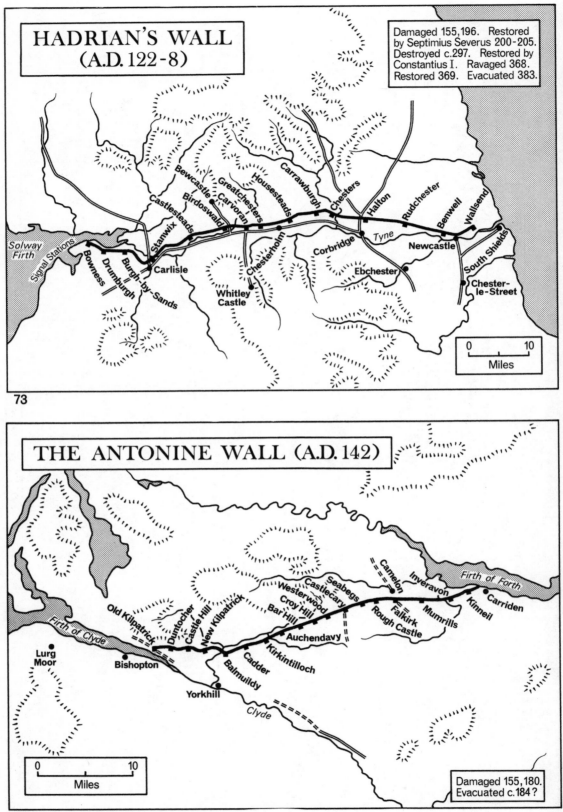

HADRIAN'S WALL
(A.D. 122-8)

Damaged 155, 196. Restored by Septimius Severus 200-205. Destroyed c.297. Restored by Constantius I. Ravaged 368. Restored 369. Evacuated 383.

Bewcastle

Greatchesters

Housesteads

Carrawburgh

Chesters

Halton

Rudchester

Benwell

Wallsend

Castlesteads

Birdoswald

Carvoran

Stanwix

Solway Firth

Signal Stations

Bowness

Drumburgh

Burgh-by-Sands

Carlisle

Chesterholm

Corbridge

Tyne

Newcastle

South Shields

Ebchester

Chester-le-Street

Whitley Castle

0   10
Miles

73

THE ANTONINE WALL (A.D. 142)

Camelon

Inveravon

Firth of Forth

Seabegs

Castlecary

Westerwood

Croy Hill

Bar Hill

Falkirk

Mumrills

Kinneil

Carriden

Old Kilpatrick

Duntocher

Castle Hill

New Kilpatrick

Rough Castle

Auchendavy

Firth of Clyde

Kirkintilloch

Lurg Moor

Bishopton

Cadder

Balmuildy

Yorkhill

Clyde

0   10
Miles

Damaged 155, 180. Evacuated c.184?

74

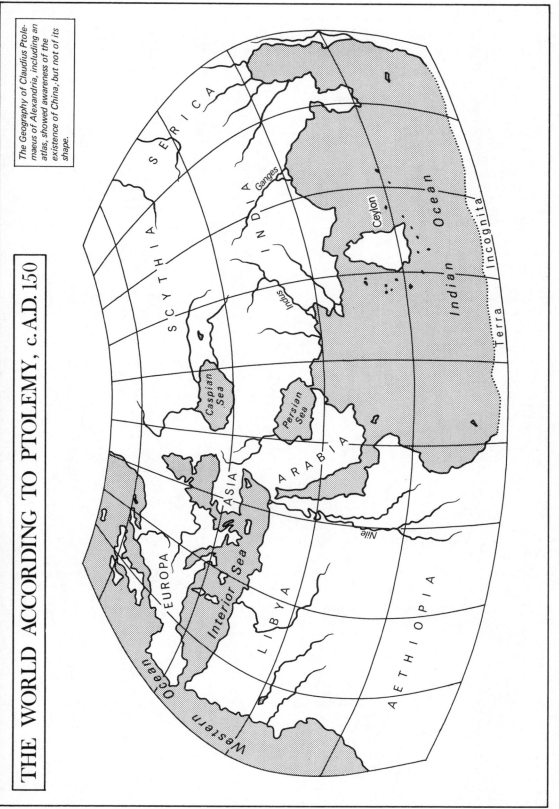

THE WORLD ACCORDING TO PTOLEMY, c. A.D. 150

The Geography of Claudius Ptolemaeus of Alexandria, including an atlas, showed awareness of the existence of China, but not of its shape.

SERICA

SCYTHIA

INDIA

Ganges

Indus

Ceylon

Indian Ocean

Terra Incognita

Caspian Sea

Persian Sea

ARABIA

ASIA

EUROPA

Interior Sea

Nile

LIBYA

AETHIOPIA

Western Ocean

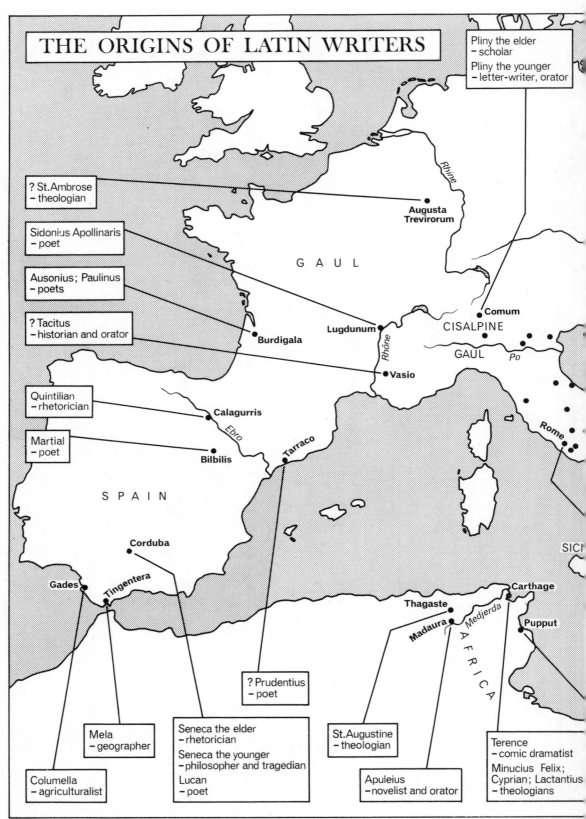

THE ORIGINS OF LATIN WRITERS

Pliny the elder
– scholar
Pliny the younger
– letter-writer, orator

? St.Ambrose
– theologian

Sidonius Apollinaris
– poet

Ausonius; Paulinus
– poets

? Tacitus
– historian and orator

Quintilian
– rhetorician

Martial
– poet

Augusta
Trevirorum

Rhine

G A U L

Comum

CISALPINE

Lugdunum

GAUL   Po

Rhône

Burdigala

Vasio

Calagurris

Ebro

Tarraco

Bilbilis

Rome

S P A I N

Corduba

SICI

Gades

Tingentera

Carthage

Thagaste

Medjerda

Pupput

Madaura

A
F
R
I
C
A

? Prudentius
– poet

Mela
– geographer

Seneca the elder
– rhetorician
Seneca the younger
– philosopher and tragedian
Lucan
– poet

St.Augustine
– theologian

Terence
– comic dramatist

Minucius Felix;
Cyprian; Lactantius
– theologians

Columella
– agriculturalist

Apuleius
– novelist and orator

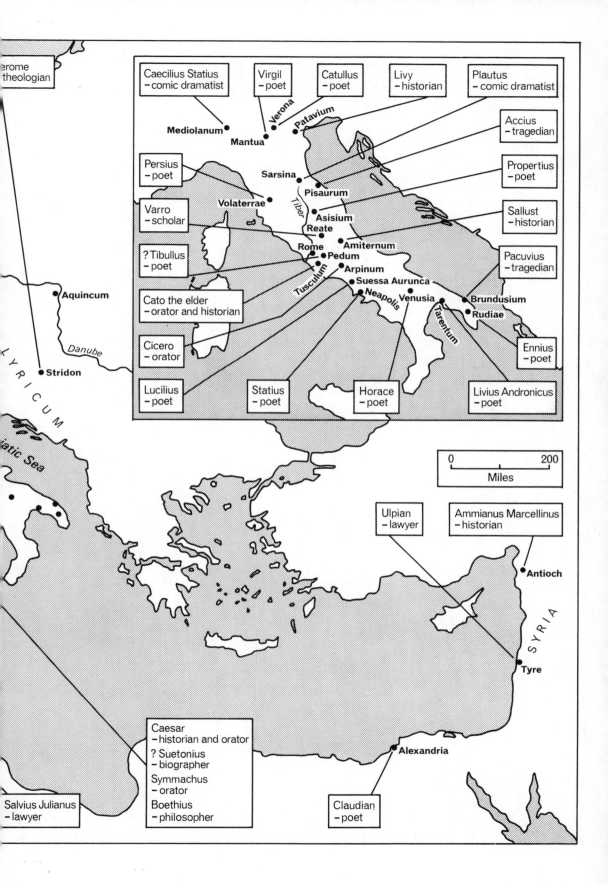

Jerome
– theologian

Caecilius Statius
– comic dramatist

Virgil
– poet

Catullus
– poet

Livy
– historian

Plautus
– comic dramatist

Accius
– tragedian

Persius
– poet

Propertius
– poet

Varro
– scholar

Sallust
– historian

?Tibullus
– poet

Pacuvius
– tragedian

Cato the elder
– orator and historian

Cicero
– orator

Ennius
– poet

Lucilius
– poet

Statius
– poet

Horace
– poet

Livius Andronicus
– poet

Ulpian
– lawyer

Ammianus Marcellinus
– historian

Caesar
– historian and orator
?Suetonius
– biographer
Symmachus
– orator
Boethius
– philosopher

Salvius Julianus
– lawyer

Claudian
– poet

Mediolanum
Mantua
Verona
Patavium
Sarsina
Pisaurum
Volaterrae
Tiber
Asisium
Reate
Amiternum
Rome
Pedum
Arpinum
Tusculum
Suessa Aurunca
Neapolis
Venusia
Brundusium
Rudiae
Tarentum

Aquincum
Stridon

ILLYRICUM
Danube

Adriatic Sea

0   200
Miles

SYRIA

Antioch
Tyre

Alexandria

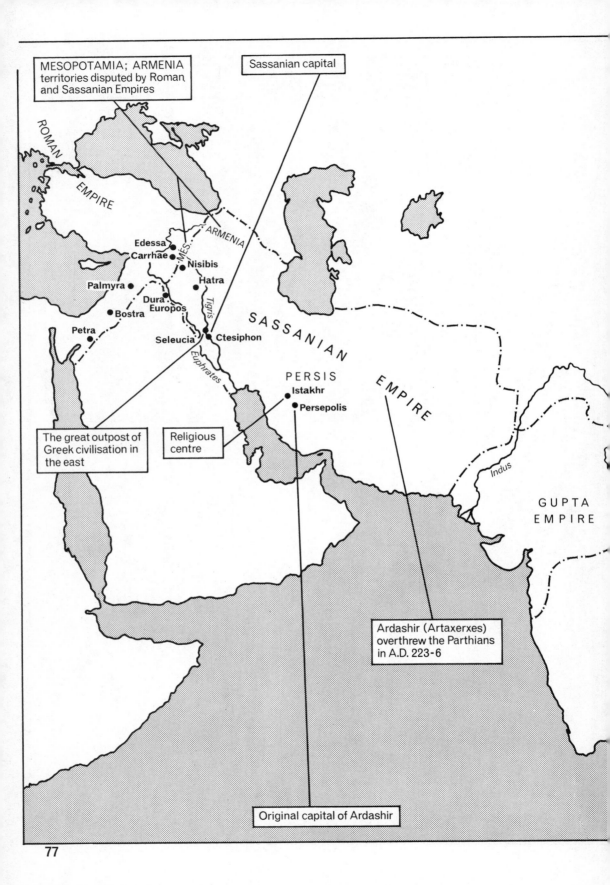

MESOPOTAMIA; ARMENIA
territories disputed by Roman
and Sassanian Empires

Sassanian capital

ROMAN

EMPIRE

ARMENIA

Edessa
Carrhae
MES.
Nisibis
Hatra
Palmyra
Dura
Europos
Bostra
Tigris
SASSANIAN
Petra
Seleucia
Ctesiphon
EMPIRE
Euphrates
PERSIS
Istakhr
Persepolis

The great outpost of
Greek civilisation in
the east

Religious
centre

Indus

GUPTA
EMPIRE

Ardashir (Artaxerxes)
overthrew the Parthians
in A.D. 223-6

Original capital of Ardashir

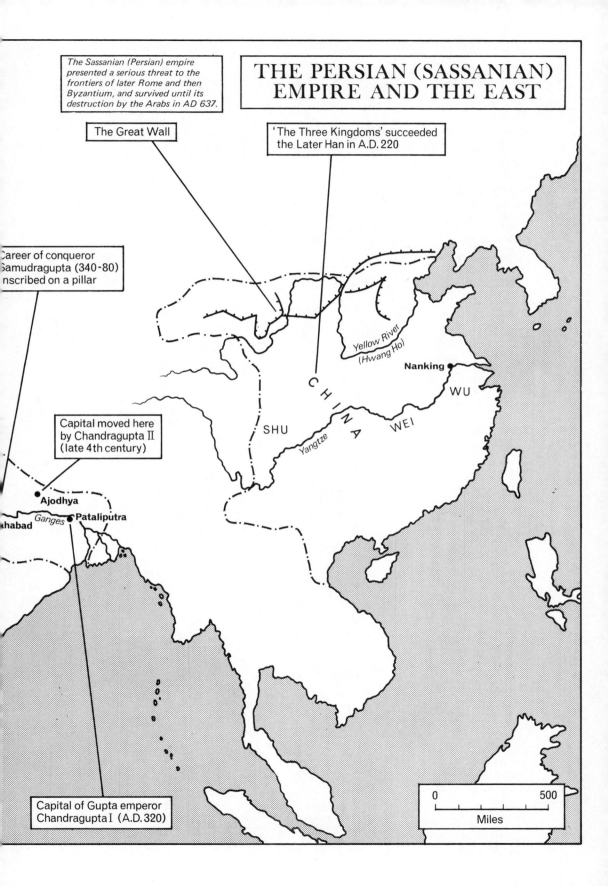

The Sassanian (Persian) empire presented a serious threat to the frontiers of later Rome and then Byzantium, and survived until its destruction by the Arabs in AD 637.

THE PERSIAN (SASSANIAN) EMPIRE AND THE EAST

The Great Wall

'The Three Kingdoms' succeeded the Later Han in A.D. 220

Career of conqueror Samudragupta (340-80) inscribed on a pillar

Capital moved here by Chandragupta II (late 4th century)

Capital of Gupta emperor Chandragupta I (A.D. 320)

Yellow River (Hwang Ho)

Nanking

C H I N A

WU

SHU

WEI

Yangtze

Ajodhya

Ganges   Pataliputra

habad

0   500

Miles

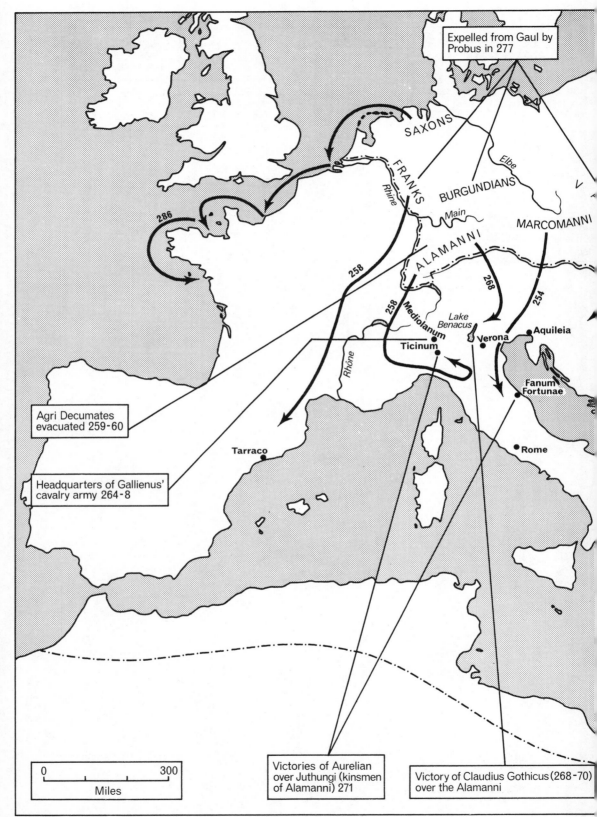

Expelled from Gaul by
Probus in 277

SAXONS

FRANKS

BURGUNDIANS

Elbe

MARCOMANNI

Main

ALAMANNI

Rhine

286

258

258

Mediolanum

Rhône

Ticinum

Lake
Benacus

Verona

268

254

Aquileia

Fanum
Fortunae

Rome

Agri Decumates
evacuated 259-60

Tarraco

Headquarters of Gallienus'
cavalry army 264-8

Victories of Aurelian
over Juthungi (kinsmen
of Alamanni) 271

Victory of Claudius Gothicus (268-70)
over the Alamanni

0   300

Miles

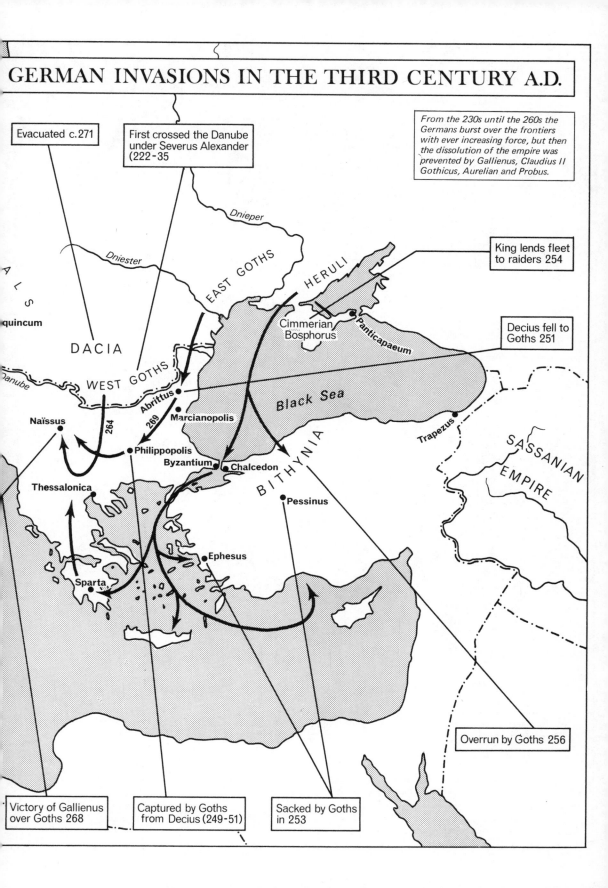

GERMAN INVASIONS IN THE THIRD CENTURY A.D.

From the 230s until the 260s the Germans burst over the frontiers with ever increasing force, but then the dissolution of the empire was prevented by Gallienus, Claudius II Gothicus, Aurelian and Probus.

Evacuated c.271

First crossed the Danube under Severus Alexander (222-35

King lends fleet to raiders 254

Decius fell to Goths 251

Overrun by Goths 256

Victory of Gallienus over Goths 268

Captured by Goths from Decius (249-51)

Sacked by Goths in 253

Dnieper

Dniester

EAST GOTHS

HERULI

quincum

DACIA

WEST GOTHS

Cimmerian Bosphorus

Panticapaeum

Danube

264

269

Abrittus

Marcianopolis

Black Sea

Naïssus

Philippopolis

Byzantium

Chalcedon

BITHYNIA

Trapezus

SASSANIAN EMPIRE

Thessalonica

Pessinus

Ephesus

Sparta

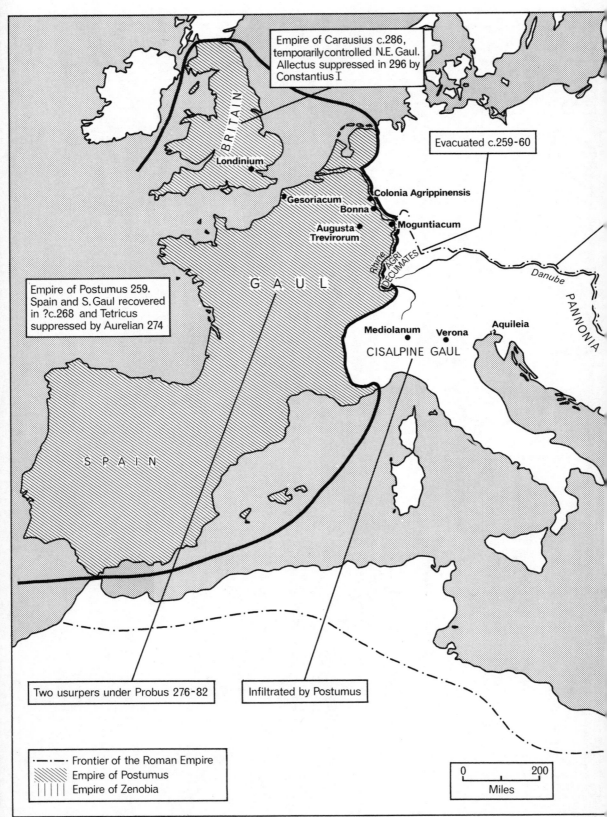

Empire of Carausius c.286,
temporarily controlled N.E. Gaul.
Allectus suppressed in 296 by
Constantius I

Evacuated c.259-60

BRITAIN

Londinium

Gesoriacum   Colonia Agrippinensis
       Bonna
    Augusta   Moguntiacum
   Trevirorum
                    Rhine AGRI
                          DECUMATES

GAUL   Danube PANNONIA

Empire of Postumus 259.
Spain and S. Gaul recovered
in ?c.268 and Tetricus
suppressed by Aurelian 274

                    Mediolanum   Verona   Aquileia

                    CISALPINE GAUL

S P A I N

Two usurpers under Probus 276-82   Infiltrated by Postumus

—·—·— Frontier of the Roman Empire
/////// Empire of Postumus
|||||| Empire of Zenobia

0   200
    Miles

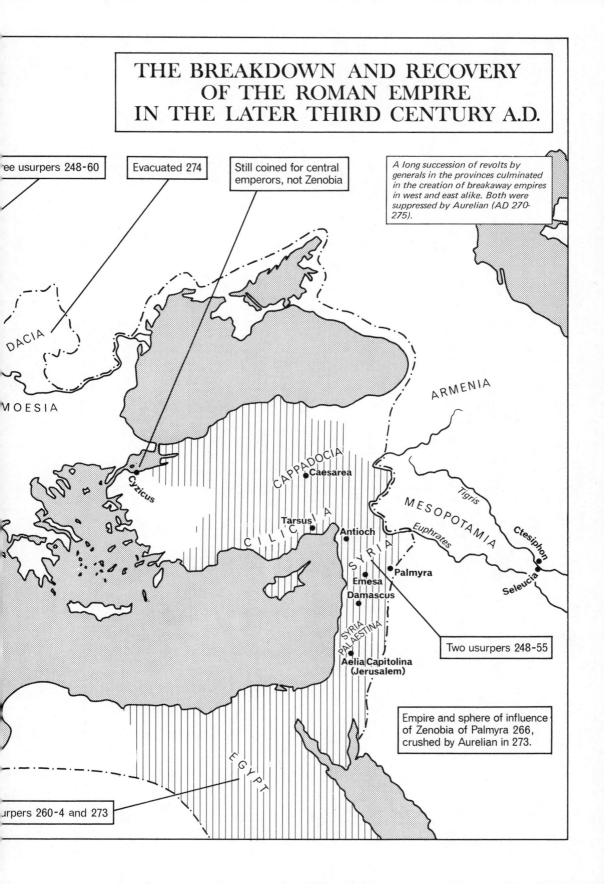

THE BREAKDOWN AND RECOVERY OF THE ROMAN EMPIRE IN THE LATER THIRD CENTURY A.D.

ree usurpers 248-60

Evacuated 274

Still coined for central emperors, not Zenobia

A long succession of revolts by generals in the provinces culminated in the creation of breakaway empires in west and east alike. Both were suppressed by Aurelian (AD 270-275).

DACIA

MOESIA

ARMENIA

CAPPADOCIA

Caesarea

MESOPOTAMIA

Tigris

Ctesiphon

Cyzicus

Tarsus

CILICIA

Antioch

Euphrates

SYRIA

Palmyra

Seleucia

Emesa

Damascus

SYRIA PALAESTINA

Two usurpers 248-55

Aelia Capitolina (Jerusalem)

Empire and sphere of influence of Zenobia of Palmyra 266, crushed by Aurelian in 273.

EGYPT

urpers 260-4 and 273

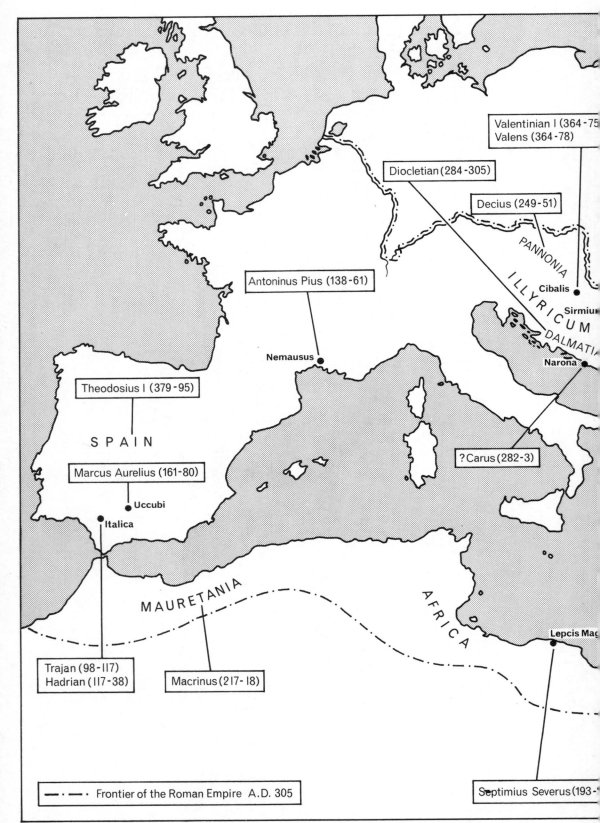

Valentinian I (364-75)
Valens (364-78)

Diocletian (284-305)

Decius (249-51)

PANNONIA

ILLYRICUM

Cibalis

Sirmium

DALMATIA

Antoninus Pius (138-61)

Narona

Nemausus

Theodosius I (379-95)

SPAIN

?Carus (282-3)

Marcus Aurelius (161-80)

Uccubi

Italica

MAURETANIA

AFRICA

Lepcis Magna

Trajan (98-117)
Hadrian (117-38)

Macrinus (217-18)

— · — Frontier of the Roman Empire A.D. 305

Septimius Severus (193-

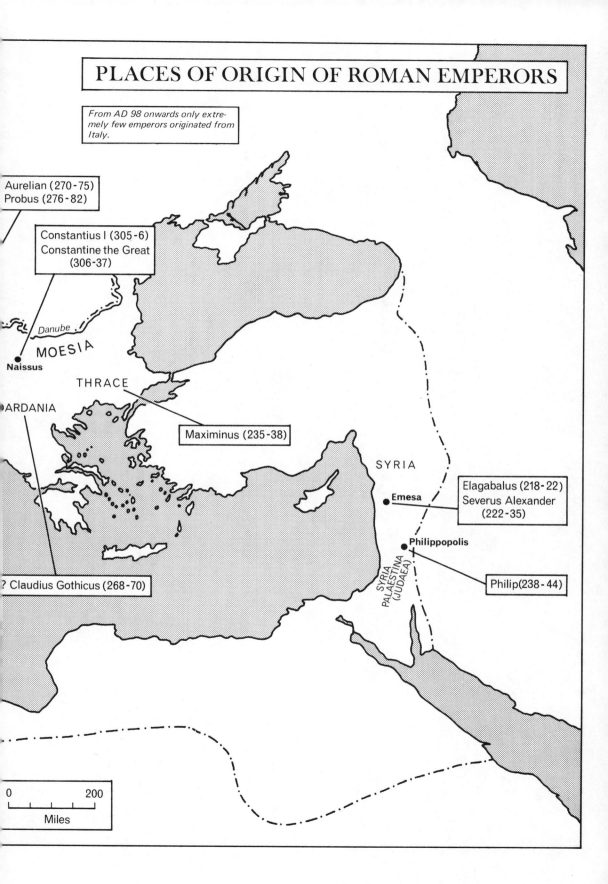

PLACES OF ORIGIN OF ROMAN EMPERORS

From AD 98 onwards only extremely few emperors originated from Italy.

Aurelian (270-75)
Probus (276-82)

Constantius I (305-6)
Constantine the Great
(306-37)

Danube

MOESIA

● **Naissus**

THRACE

ARDANIA

Maximinus (235-38)

SYRIA

Elagabalus (218-22)
Severus Alexander
(222-35)

● **Emesa**

● **Philippopolis**

SYRIA
PALAESTINA
(JUDAEA)

Philip(238-44)

? Claudius Gothicus (268-70)

0   200

Miles

GERMANIA

Colonia

Rhine

Regina

Aquincum

PANNONIA

Mursa

Lutetia

Genabum

Vesontio

Alps

Tergeste

Ravenna

DALMATIA

Genua

ITALY

APULIA

Burdigala

Tolosa

Pyrenees

Massilia

Rome

CALAB

CAMPANIA

G A U L

S P A I N

SARDINIA

Caralis

Panormus

SICILY

Jews deported from
Rome by Tiberius
A.D. 14 - 37

Corduba

Gades

Carthage

Melita

Volubilis

Atlas Mountains

S A H A R A

Oea

0   250

Miles

■ Areas of widespread Jewish settlement
● Towns with large Jewish communities

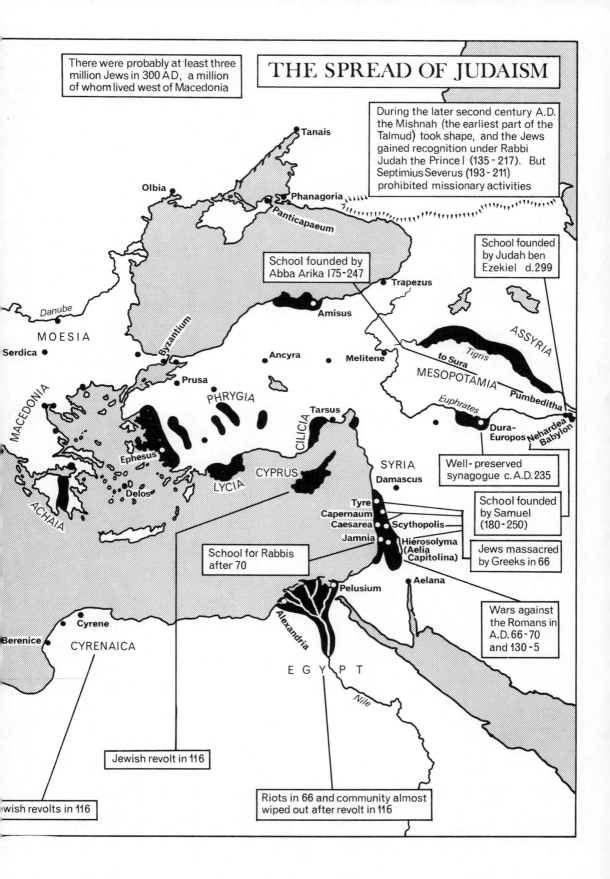

THE SPREAD OF JUDAISM

There were probably at least three million Jews in 300 A.D., a million of whom lived west of Macedonia

During the later second century A.D. the Mishnah (the earliest part of the Talmud) took shape, and the Jews gained recognition under Rabbi Judah the Prince I (135 - 217). But Septimius Severus (193 - 211) prohibited missionary activities

Tanais

Olbia

Phanagoria

Panticapaeum

School founded by Judah ben Ezekiel d.299

School founded by Abba Arika 175 - 247

Trapezus

ASSYRIA

Danube

Amisus

Tigris

MOESIA

to Sura

Serdica

Ancyra

Melitene

MESOPOTAMIA

Pumbeditha

Byzantium

Prusa

Euphrates

PHRYGIA

Tarsus

Dura-Euryopos

Nehardea
Babylon

MACEDONIA

CILICIA

Ephesus

CYPRUS

SYRIA

Well-preserved synagogue c. A.D. 235

LYCIA

Damascus

Delos

Tyre

School founded by Samuel (180 - 250)

ACHAIA

Capernaum

Caesarea

Scythopolis

Jamnia

Hierosolyma (Aelia Capitolina)

Jews massacred by Greeks in 66

School for Rabbis after 70

Pelusium

Aelana

Wars against the Romans in A.D. 66 - 70 and 130 - 5

Cyrene

Alexandria

Berenice

CYRENAICA

E G Y P T

Nile

Jewish revolt in 116

wish revolts in 116

Riots in 66 and community almost wiped out after revolt in 116

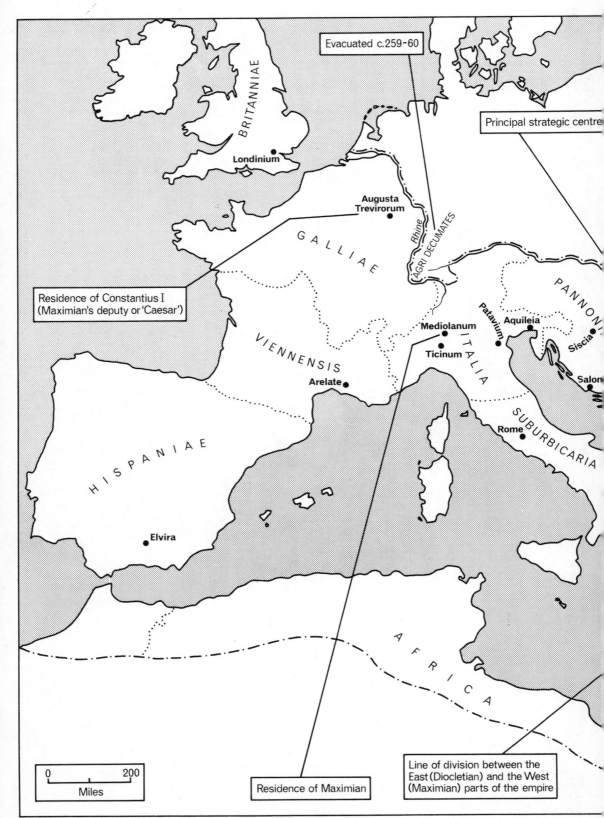

Evacuated c.259-60

Principal strategic centre

BRITANNIAE

Londinium

GALLIAE

Rhine

(AGRI DECUMATES)

PANNONI

Residence of Constantius I
(Maximian's deputy or 'Caesar')

Augusta
Trevirorum

VIENNENSIS

Mediolanum

Patavium

Aquileia

Siscia

ITALIA

Ticinum

Arelate

HISPANIAE

Rome

SUBURBICARIA

Salon

Elvira

AFRICA

0   200
Miles

Residence of Maximian

Line of division between the
East (Diocletian) and the West
(Maximian) parts of the empire

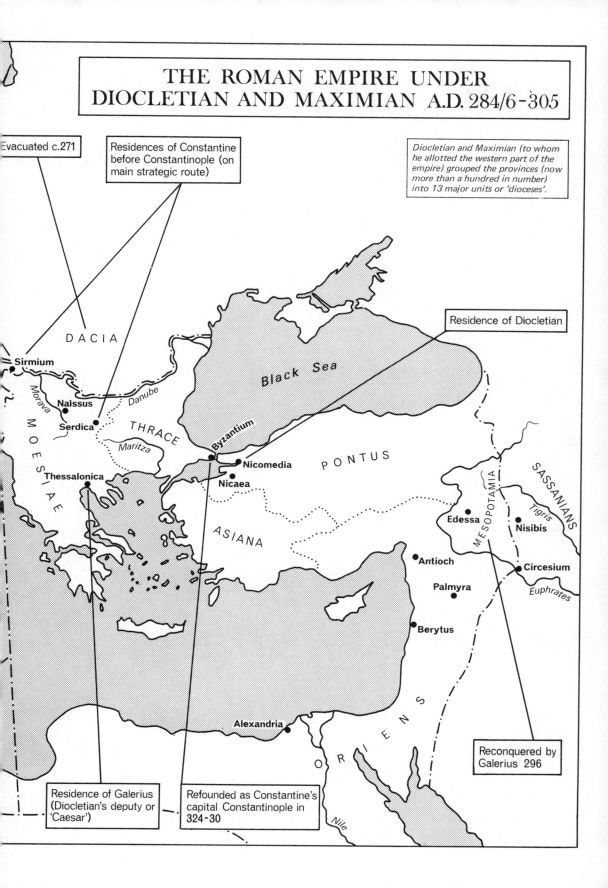

THE ROMAN EMPIRE UNDER DIOCLETIAN AND MAXIMIAN A.D. 284/6-305

Evacuated c.271

Residences of Constantine before Constantinople (on main strategic route)

Diocletian and Maximian (to whom he allotted the western part of the empire) grouped the provinces (now more than a hundred in number) into 13 major units or 'dioceses'.

Residence of Diocletian

DACIA

Black Sea

■ Sirmium

Morava

Danube

● Naissus

Serdica

THRACE

Maritza

● Byzantium

PONTUS

MESOPOTAMIA

SASSANIANS

Tigris

● Thessalonica

● Nicomedia

● Nicaea

● Edessa

● Nisibis

ASIANA

● Antioch

● Circesium

● Palmyra

Euphrates

● Berytus

● Alexandria

ORIENS

Nile

Reconquered by Galerius 296

Residence of Galerius (Diocletian's deputy or 'Caesar')

Refounded as Constantine's capital Constantinople in 324-30

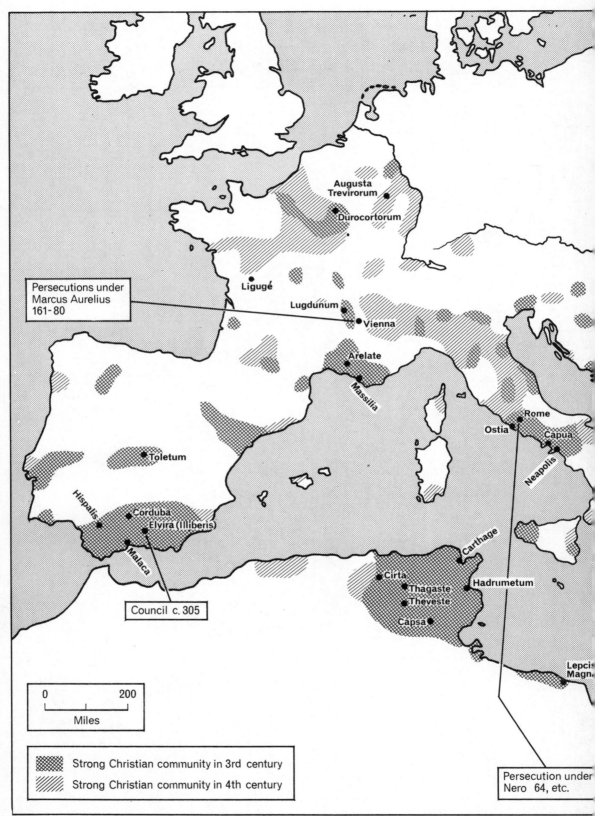

Persecutions under
Marcus Aurelius
161-80

Augusta
Trevirorum

Durocortorum

Ligugé

Lugdunum

Vienna

Arelate

Massilia

Rome

Ostia

Capua

Neapolis

Toletum

Hispalis

Corduba

Elvira (Illiberis)

Malaca

Council c. 305

Carthage

Cirta

Thagaste

Hadrumetum

Theveste

Capsa

Lepcis
Magna

0   200

Miles

Strong Christian community in 3rd century

Strong Christian community in 4th century

Persecution under
Nero 64, etc.

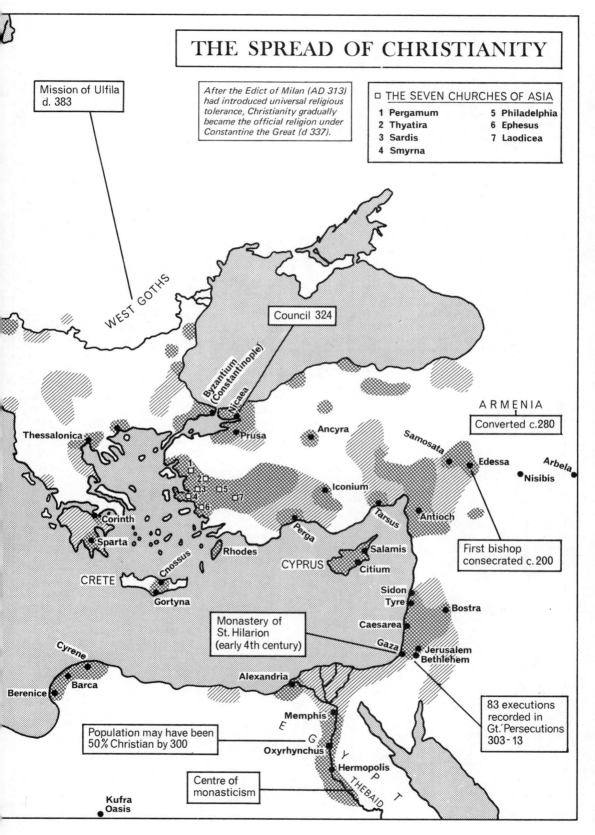

THE SPREAD OF CHRISTIANITY

Mission of Ulfila
d. 383

*After the Edict of Milan (AD 313)
had introduced universal religious
tolerance, Christianity gradually
became the official religion under
Constantine the Great (d 337).*

☐ THE SEVEN CHURCHES OF ASIA

1 Pergamum	5 Philadelphia
2 Thyatira	6 Ephesus
3 Sardis	7 Laodicea
4 Smyrna	

WEST GOTHS

Council 324

Byzantium (Constantinople)
Nicaea

ARMENIA
Converted c.280

Thessalonica

Prusa

Ancyra

Samosata

Edessa

Arbela

Nisibis

1
2
3 5
4 7
6

Iconium

Tarsus

Antioch

First bishop
consecrated c.200

Corinth

Perga

Sparta

Rhodes

Salamis

CYPRUS

Citium

CRETE

Cnossus

Sidon

Tyre

Bostra

Gortyna

Caesarea

Monastery of
St. Hilarion
(early 4th century)

Gaza

Jerusalem
Bethlehem

Cyrene

Barca

Berenice

Alexandria

83 executions
recorded in
Gt. Persecutions
303 - 13

Memphis

E

Population may have been
50% Christian by 300

G

Oxyrhynchus

Y

Centre of
monasticism

Hermopolis

P

THEBAID

T

Kufra
Oasis

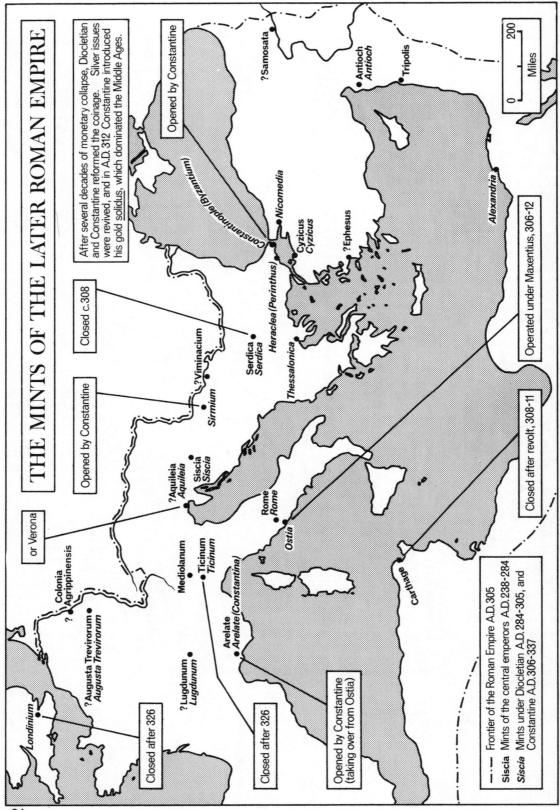

THE MINTS OF THE LATER ROMAN EMPIRE

After several decades of monetary collapse, Diocletian and Constantine reformed the coinage. Silver issues were revived, and in A.D. 312 Constantine introduced his gold solidus, which dominated the Middle Ages.

Opened by Constantine

Closed c.308

Opened by Constantine

or Verona

Closed after 326

Closed after 326

Opened by Constantine (taking over from Ostia)

Operated under Maxentius, 306-12

Closed after revolt, 308-11

Londinium

?Augusta Trevirorum
Augusta Trevirorum

Colonia Agrippinensis

?

?Lugdunum
Lugdunum

Mediolanum

Ticinum
Ticinum

Arelate
Arelate (Constantina)

Rome
Rome

Ostia

?Aquileia
Aquileia

Siscia
Siscia

Sirmium

?Viminacium

Serdica
Serdica

Thessalonica

Heraclea (Perinthus)

Constantinople (Byzantium)

Nicomedia

Cyzicus
Cyzicus

?Ephesus

?Samosata

Antioch
Antioch

Tripolis

Alexandria

Carthage

0   200
Miles

— · — Frontier of the Roman Empire A.D.305

Siscia   Mints of the central emperors A.D.238-284

Siscia Mints under Diocletian A.D. 284-305, and Constantine A.D.306-337

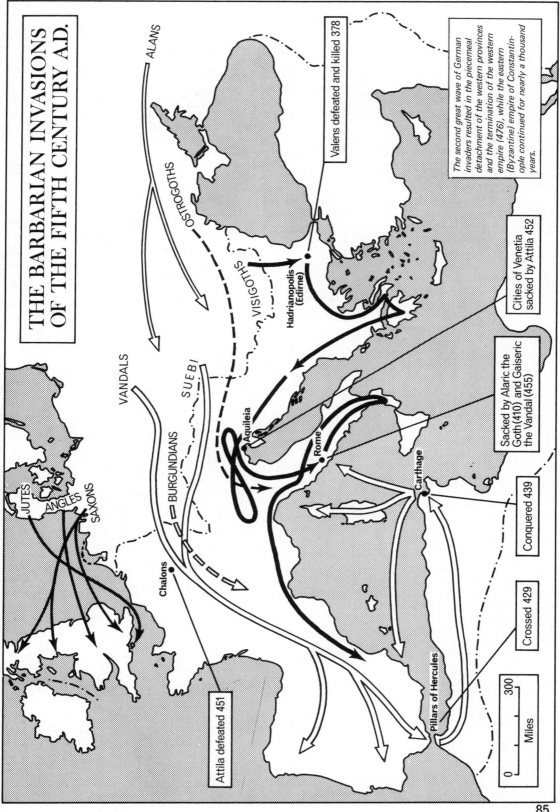

THE BARBARIAN INVASIONS OF THE FIFTH CENTURY A.D.

ALANS

OSTROGOTHS

VISIGOTHS

VANDALS

SUEBI

BURGUNDIANS

JUTES

ANGLES

SAXONS

Hadrianopolis (Edirne)

Aquileia

Rome

Carthage

Chalons

Pillars of Hercules

Valens defeated and killed 378

Cities of Venetia sacked by Attila 452

Sacked by Alaric the Goth (410) and Gaiseric the Vandal (455)

Conquered 439

Crossed 429

Attila defeated 451

The second great wave of German invaders resulted in the piecemeal detachment of the western provinces and the termination of the western empire (476), while the eastern (Byzantine) empire of Constantinople continued for nearly a thousand years.

0 — 300

Miles

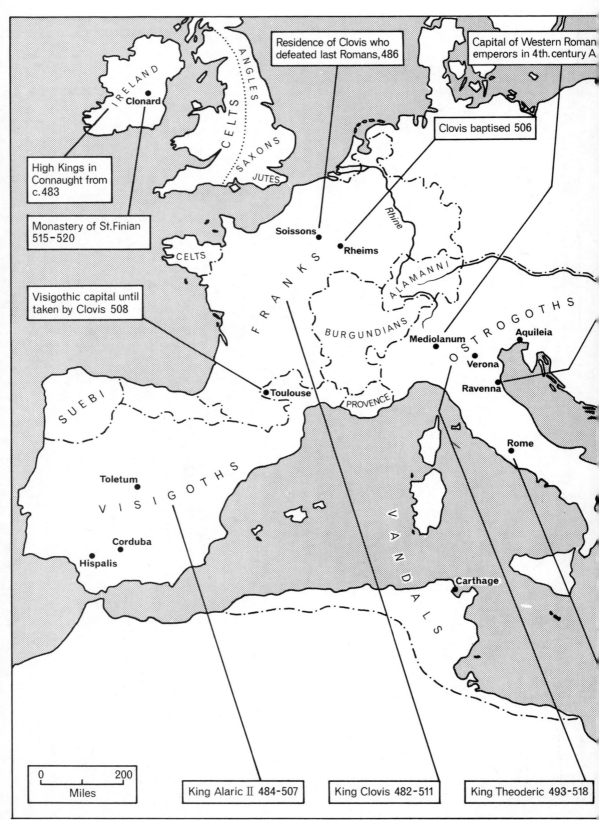

High Kings in Connaught from c.483

Monastery of St.Finian 515–520

Residence of Clovis who defeated last Romans, 486

Capital of Western Roman emperors in 4th. century A

Clovis baptised 506

Visigothic capital until taken by Clovis 508

IRELAND

Clonard

CELTS

ANGLES

SAXONS

JUTES

CELTS

FRANKS

Soissons

Rheims

Rhine

ALAMANNI

BURGUNDIANS

Mediolanum

OSTROGOTHS

Aquileia

Verona

Ravenna

Toulouse

PROVENCE

Rome

SUEBI

VISIGOTHS

Toletum

Corduba

Hispalis

VANDALS

Carthage

0   200
Miles

King Alaric II 484–507

King Clovis 482–511

King Theoderic 493–518

86

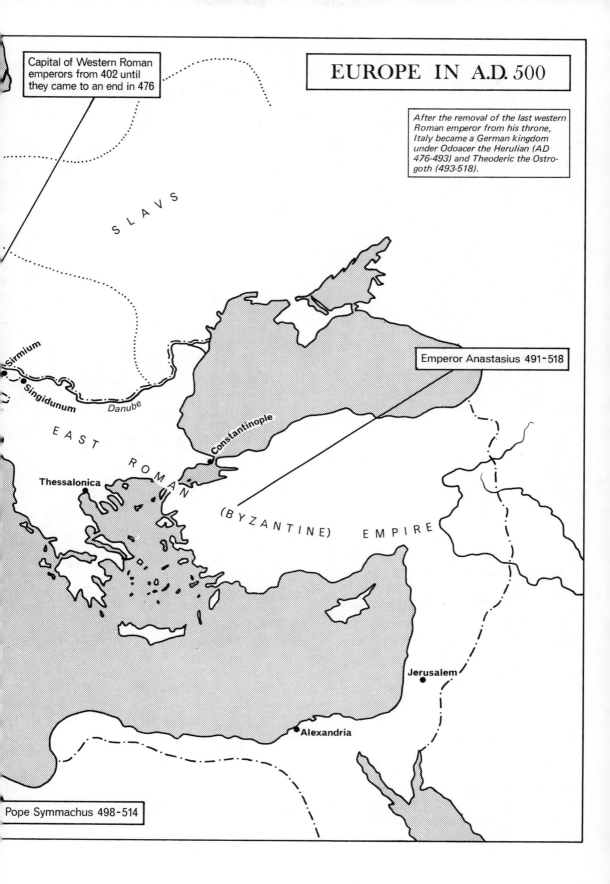

Capital of Western Roman emperors from 402 until they came to an end in 476

EUROPE IN A.D. 500

After the removal of the last western Roman emperor from his throne, Italy became a German kingdom under Odoacer the Herulian (AD 476-493) and Theoderic the Ostrogoth (493-518).

S L A V S

Sirmium

Singidunum

Danube

E A S T

R O M A N

Emperor Anastasius 491-518

Constantinople

Thessalonica

(B Y Z A N T I N E)   E M P I R E

Jerusalem

Alexandria

Pope Symmachus 498-514

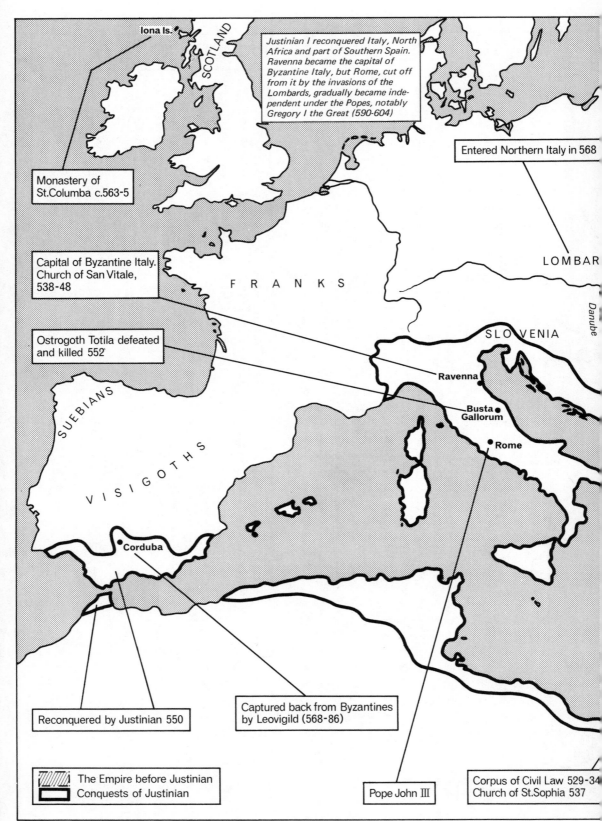

Iona Is.

SCOTLAND

Justinian I reconquered Italy, North
Africa and part of Southern Spain.
Ravenna became the capital of
Byzantine Italy, but Rome, cut off
from it by the invasions of the
Lombards, gradually became inde-
pendent under the Popes, notably
Gregory I the Great (590-604)

Entered Northern Italy in 568

Monastery of
St.Columba c.563-5

LOMBAR

Danube

Capital of Byzantine Italy.
Church of San Vitale,
538-48

F R A N K S

S L O V E N I A

Ostrogoth Totila defeated
and killed 552

Ravenna

Busta
Gallorum

SUEBIANS

Rome

V I S I G O T H S

Corduba

Reconquered by Justinian 550

Captured back from Byzantines
by Leovigild (568-86)

The Empire before Justinian
Conquests of Justinian

Pope John III

Corpus of Civil Law 529-34
Church of St.Sophia 537

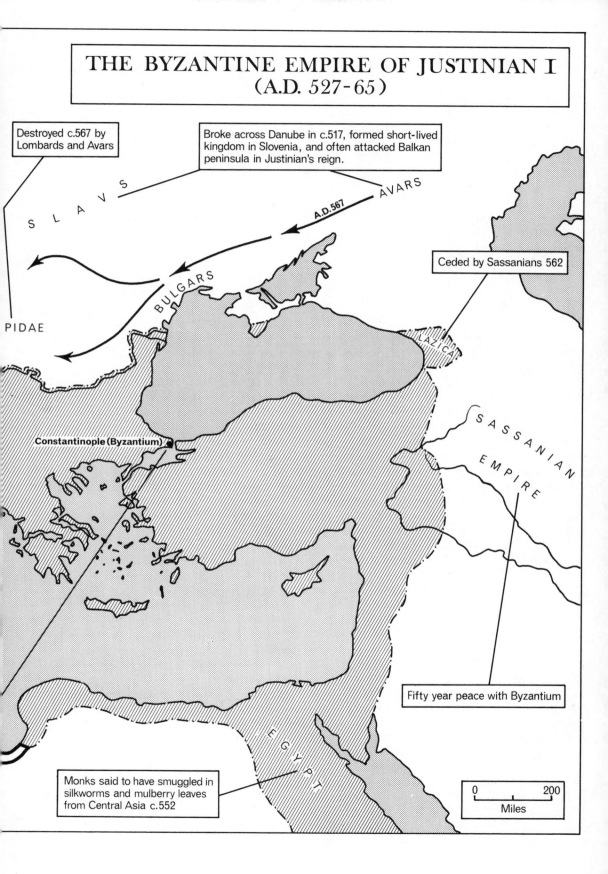

THE BYZANTINE EMPIRE OF JUSTINIAN I
(A.D. 527-65)

Destroyed c.567 by
Lombards and Avars

Broke across Danube in c.517, formed short-lived
kingdom in Slovenia, and often attacked Balkan
peninsula in Justinian's reign.

S L A V S

AVARS

A.D. 567

BULGARS

PIDAE

Ceded by Sassanians 562

LAZICA

Constantinople (Byzantium)

S A S S A N I A N

E M P I R E

Fifty year peace with Byzantium

E G Y P T

Monks said to have smuggled in
silkworms and mulberry leaves
from Central Asia c.552

0   200
Miles

Index of Place Names[1]

Modern names are given in brackets

[1] I have sometimes sacrificed consistency of spelling to convenience and tradition.

MAR 1 8 1994